EXTREME

For Emile, Mason and Avery,
in extreme

First published in the United Kingdom in 2009 by Thames & Hudson Ltd,
181A High Holborn, London WC1V 7QX

www.thamesandhudson.com

British Library Cataloguing-in-Publication Data
A catalogue record for this book is available from the British Library

ISBN 978-0-500-34251-0

Designed by Grade Design Consultants
Printed and bound in China by C&C Offset Printing Co Ltd

Phyllis Richardson

XS Extreme:
Big Ideas,
Small Buildings

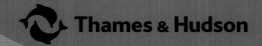

Thames & Hudson

art and craft

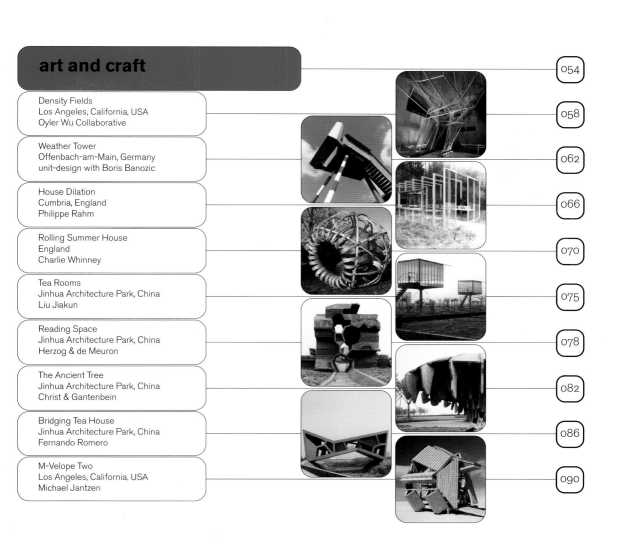

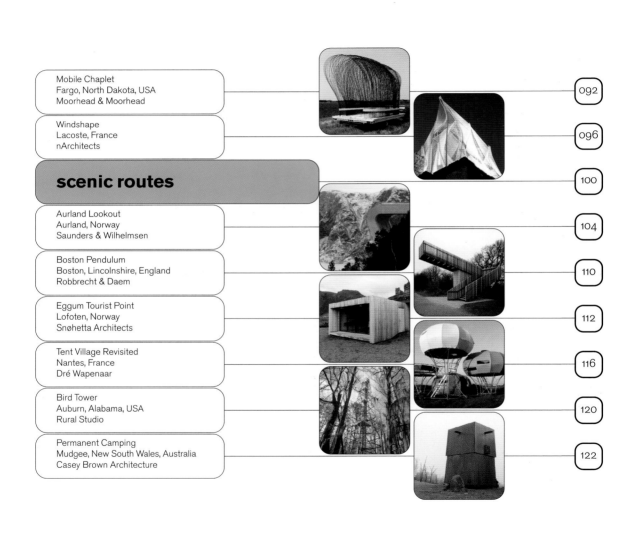

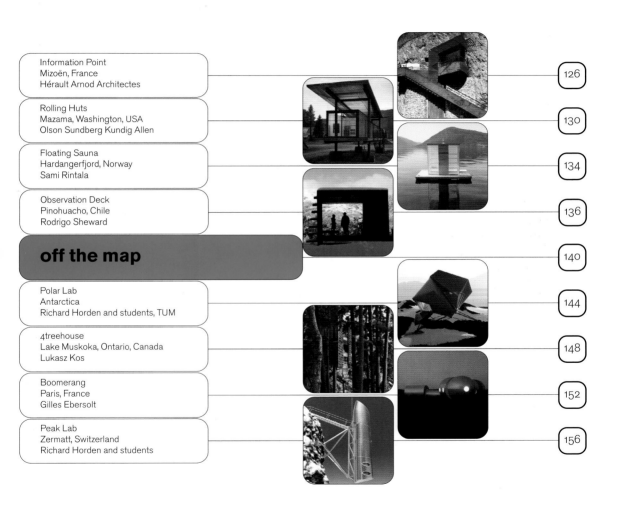

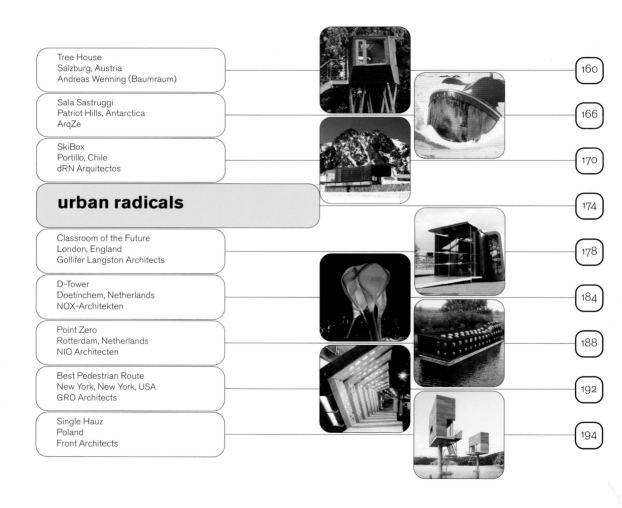

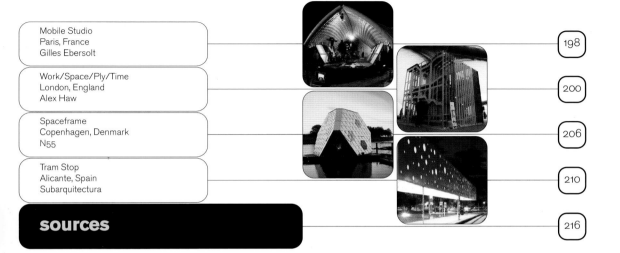

Introduction

beyond boundaries

'Every great action is extreme', François de la Rochefoucauld

When conceiving the idea of the XS series, we were always looking for buildings that were exceptional, experimental, and in some ways extreme. As architects and designers continue to experiment with building forms on a small scale, the series has carried on, examining more specific areas of research and innovation. The previous volume, XS Green, was devoted to small buildings that embraced the ecological imperative. This, the third volume, looks at the work of those who are stretching definitions, perceptions and expectations, as well as, in a more literal sense, material performance, site specificity and/or function.

To celebrate extreme buildings is to consider those types and models that achieve beyond what is expected of mere shelter, beyond even what we have come to expect from the unusual, or even whimsical. For it is sometimes in the most outlandish ideas that the kernel of a new possibility is found and allowed to take root, resulting in more useful and efficient materials and methods. It is also worthwhile to look at the extremes in order to remind ourselves of what is already possible, though not commonplace, and of how infrequently we encounter design on any scale that questions received notions of acceptable building practice. These are not only

structures that are wildly anomalous, but those that quietly warrant a second look, which may lead to a third and perhaps even a detour from our routine trajectory in order to investigate something that has managed to pique our too-dormant curiosity in the built environment.

In this book, 'extreme' is used to refer to different aspects of building. The projects that feature in the first chapter represent experiments with materials that are either the result of technologically advanced fabrication methods or newly minted composites. Here, employing new materials also means using a familiar medium in a way that is unconventional and moving towards a better or more efficient application. Surface materials are always imbued with greater significance when used on a small scale. The tactile quality of even common cladding, such as wood or concrete, has an immediate impact at the micro level that is easily lost on the vast canvas of a large building wall. At this scale, the inherent qualities and potential of innovative materials are tangible to the user if sometimes directly provocative.

The second chapter considers boundaries imposed from psychological or metaphorical understanding, the idea of distinguishing between art and architecture. These limits have to do, in the simplest differentiation, with whether a structure is counted as shelter (architecture) or sculpture (art). The debate is something of a modern construct. Bramante, Vasari and Michelangelo probably never fretted over the appropriate title for those who studied and practised the fine arts and yet supervised one of the most ambitious building projects in history, but we have cultivated the distinction with the advanced expertise of engineering. Yet, with advances in computerized design programs and milling techniques, the artist may once again play a stronger role in the realized shape of buildings, as well as in their initial conception. In these pages, there are projects that deliberately hover in the margins between art and architecture. But if Goethe and the early 19th-century philosopher Schelling were speaking any truth when they said that 'architecture can be viewed as petrified music', then surely structure that advances to sculpture has a worth beyond shelter or art alone.

In this volume, 'extreme' also refers to geographic limits. Chapter 3 considers the physical boundaries of site and climate in buildings that are meant to bring people out into the landscape with the least possible obstacle

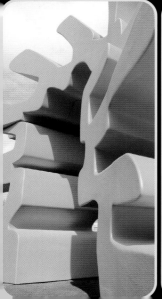

between shelter and nature. To do this, these structures not only make themselves small, but are used in places where their surroundings are of an awesome grandeur, and the contrast in scale between the natural and the man-made allows nature a righteous supremacy.

Going even further into nature, buildings designed for use in the more extreme regions of the Earth have specific demands. Chapter 4 focuses on small buildings that are suited to these environments for all kinds of reasons, including, as always, being a manageable scale for research into new ways of creating protective shelter.

These are structures whose primary challenge is to negotiate, or touch only lightly, the very ground beneath their feet. Here, the necessity of making a permanent structure on a particular site comes into question. Many of these buildings are designed to be temporary and to move from site to site without affecting the integrity of the structure. Ruskin said: 'When we build we should think that we build forever.' He couldn't conceive of a time or condition when we would want to leave no trace upon the landscape. And yet the demands of the environment and the opportunity of new materials presents a category of

temporary building that is of growing importance in our collective habitation of the Earth.

Back in the cities, buildings that enhance or improve the urban environment are perhaps of most immediate concern to the general population. As cities grow and as planning fails to make the most efficient use of finite space, the urban scene becomes less salubrious, while at the same time a necessary daily experience. Extreme approaches to the city, as featured in Chapter 5, are mostly flexible and sympathetic to the needs of people who seem to gain anonymity and lose out on humane provision as their numbers increase.

In these pages, and throughout the chapters, the extreme inspires another term of transcending boundaries: exuberance. There is something celebratory about a mountain lookout that casts an open view over the landscape, a mobile meditation space that resembles the free-form nature of the surrounding prairie grass, a pod designed for polar exploration. They signify the boundlessness of the human imagination, and in the great Renaissance tradition, the refusal to be proscribed by categories, the limits of current technology, or by predetermined ambitions. In this the extreme becomes for most of us a necessary exercise in optimism.

new and improved

Innovative materials and structural solutions

The modern movement could be defined as the search for and implementation of the best new materials for the most efficient use of space, light and energy. Or that could just be the aim of good building practice. Sometimes new materials are just that, something never before seen in the world, a new grade of synthetic used in a specially developed double-wall system, such as that employed for Kengo Kuma's Tea House. As an architect more known for his poetic forms in wood, Kuma also exhibits an admirable knack for innovation. Here, the structure is inflatable to minimize its impact on the environment, leaving behind almost no evidence of its existence. The double-walled system makes it more resistant to wind and temperature change.

Temperate conditions, or the lack of them, inspired Monika Gora's Glass Bubble, designed for the particularly harsh conditions on the Swedish coast, which creates a tropical microclimate for a variety of plants. Materially and geometrically complex, the structure required new 3D software to create shapes that were then coaxed into being with the use of extremely thin bent-glass panels, after other forms of glass were considered and dismissed.

In his contribution to the British seaside resort, Ian McChesney decided to embrace and make the best use of the local weather conditions. His weathervane/shelter is constructed from a steel alloy developed to resist corrosion, and an aerodynamic shape designed not to reduce wind drag, but to use it to full effect. For the comfort of those sheltering within, his elegantly twisting structure turns with every blast to keep its protective back to the strong coastal breeze.

German group SMAQ also looked to the skies to inform an open-air public bathing pavilion that uses a stretch of plastic hose as both structure and thermal system. As water runs through the sculptural assemblage, it is heated by the sun before entering the pool. While both the tubing (reminiscent of the garden hose) and the decking (recalling beachside walkways) are familiar materials, they have been brought together in a surprising and surprisingly effective way.

A striking combination of a different sort is in the 'kinetic' architecture of Najjar & Najjar, who created an insectoidal shape that responds to the movement of the person inside and offers a protected viewing space for the hermit in all of us. And Gin Johannes continues to explore the possibilities of hand-welded iron framework, lighting effects and 'jelly' material. Jelly architecture may have a visual affinity with the sea creature, but the architect is more concerned with the human form and emotions, as changeable as those may be.

While such feats of technology may question the achievement of less reflexive materials, there is still some wonder to be had in a wedding chapel that eschews colonial masonry for glass panels in Mexico, or a whimsical sculpture created as a gateway to an art festival. Jürgen Mayer's bold, playful Beat Wave is an experiment in material and form, and its polystyrofoam structure demonstrates the point that a material revolution is sometimes about using existing materials in an unexpected way, asking us whether we really have exhausted the possibilities of what we already know or think we know.

Jack Woolley certainly felt that there was more to material than meets the eye when he decided to create a structure from 600 crisp packets. Though also a statement about the plague of discarded rubbish, his project poses the reinvigorated question about one man's rubbish being another man's moisture-resistant building material.

crazy beat
Beat Wave
Miami, Florida, USA
J. Mayer H.

Stuttgart-born Jürgen Mayer has raised a lot of eyebrows both within and without the architecture community, not just for the quirky forms he conceives, but also for the fact that he has managed to build so many of them, and at such a young age. Rather than chase stardom in the booming economies of the Far East or in the vast new Arab developments, Mayer has nurtured projects in his home country and in Europe, where he has explored the possibilities of the 'blob' and gone far beyond it, both technically and artistically. In addition to his predilection for stretched or patterned organic shapes, such as the 'semi-forest/semi-skeleton' of his student canteen in Karlsruhe, Mayer also integrates interactive technology into his buildings. His first signature structure, the Stadt.Haus in Stuttgart, featured a virtual screen made from 'pitter-patterns', or 'computer-generated rain', projected from the building and through which visitors must pass to enter.

Beat Wave is a small, whimsical addition to an oeuvre already populated with unusual shapes and artful dynamism. The playful structure, created as an entrance arch to the 2007 PULSE Contemporary Art Fair in Miami, is made from polystyrofoam with a polyurethane coating. It was produced using three-dimensional CAD modelling and CNC technology. Appearing like a cartoon graphic of a rippling wave, it is an instant landmark, interjecting a joyful note against the existing buildings. The arch also acts as a seating area and, of course, as an immediately recognizable meeting point.

In his work, Mayer 'strategically chooses to bypass architecture and to use art as an operative platform'. Unlike

his larger municipal works, which all have much more complex programmatic functions, Beat Wave, it seems, also offered the chance to focus more wholeheartedly on the structure as art. (In fact, it now stands in the garden of a private collector near San Francisco.) It is one more example of the offerings of a wide-ranging talent that hints at the yet more extreme (unusual, weird and wonderful?) projects that are still to come.

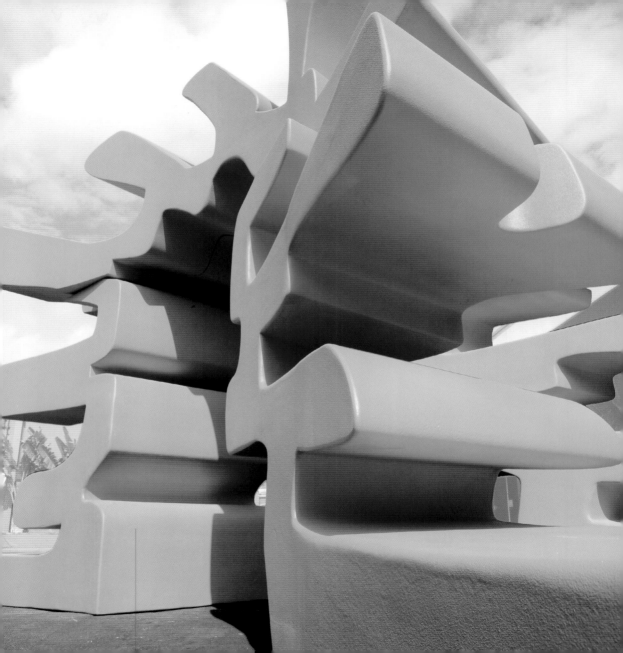

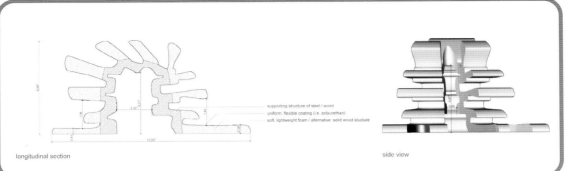

longitudinal section

supporting structure of steel / wood
uniform, flexible coating (i.e. polyurethan)
soft, lightweight foam / alternative: solid wood stucture

side view

[above] The section and elevation reveal the balance of protrusions and indentations, the way the shapes are 'cantilevering, split and sliced'.
[right and opposite] The feet of the structure provide seating for visitors to the art fair, while the arch makes a bold entrance gate.

'[The idea was] to find a very particular form, never seen before, which interacts with the people, as seating, meeting point …'

home alone

Bug
Vienna, Austria
Najjar & Najjar

Brothers Karim and Rames Najjar set up their practice in Vienna in 1999, and since then have executed a range of designs from naval architecture to commercial buildings, to villas and their beloved 'research' projects. It is easy to see them as brothers constantly playing with structures and forms, and their built work exudes an energetic enthusiasm for stretching angles and refining elements. There is something, too, of the fascination with natural forms. They might as easily take on the shape and movement of a jellyfish as an insectoidal form, and then add elegant, rhythmic fenestration, a series of supports that from a distance resembles an exoskeleton, all hard shell underpinned with a more delicate arrangement.

Karim and Rames also have a penchant for sharp, obtuse angles that convey a real sense of dynamism. It is no surprise then to see their sleek designs of narrow, pointed profiles for yachts that seem much more about speed, a smooth arrow darting through the water, as about luxurious interiors. That fascination with movement is indulged in their research, to which they dedicate a significant portion of their time and energy, and their experimentation with what they place under the rubric 'kinematic structures'.

The Bug is one of several such structures that the brothers have produced in their efforts to combine building with movement. According to the architects, 'the envelope is an instrument of communication — it changes its structure according to the events that occur inside'. The structure can support one person, and as he moves, it shifts its centre of gravity to stabilize itself, and in some ways to express something about the person housed inside.

The Bug is a philosophical exploration that strives to 'visualize the solitude of man in his environment'. In the same way that a hermit, in his seclusion, can have an impact on society by the fact that people know he exists, the Bug allows a person to be separate from the world, but since his movements are echoed in the shifting of the structure, he is still visible and in the world as the box changes shape.

The mechanism that allows the Bug to change from one balanced state to another is an arrangement of 'articulated parallelograms', planes and hinges. As Karim and Rames put it, it is like 'a struggle of architectural objects trying to escape their static shape'. Playfulness is there, but also a sense of being distanced from the physical world while still being able to confirm your existence in it.

[below] 'We chose an icon to start with: a simple box,' the architects say. Box 1 remains closed and moves within the structure of Box 2, as the centre of gravity changes with the person moving inside. Meanwhile, the outer structure, Box 2, can break up and unfold, allowing the viewer glimspes of the activity within.

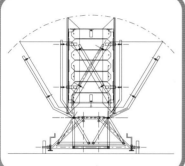

[opposite] When Karim and Rames went to build a full-scale prototype, they found that the kinetic construction of the two boxes was foiling the hull. So they developed a 'smart hull' out of aluminium panels that shift to reduce or enlarge the surface and to adjust to the primary surface. Some of the panels are translucent mesh, while others remain opaque.

'Maybe an analogy is to a medieval hermitage or …
a boy hiding in a treetop.'

hot tub
Bad (Bath)
Stuttgart, Germany
SMAQ

Sabine Müller and Andreas Quednau liken this 2006 project to the childhood experience of drawing warm water from a garden hose that has been left in the sun. Knowing this makes one look at their outdoor bathing structure with a more attuned eye. It's a hose, yes, coiled and draped and woven over the top of a wooden structure that is also reminiscent of summer – sun decks, piers, beach huts, hot tubs. The hose is one thousand metres in length, so it has a lot of twisting to do. But the sculptural form is not accidental or for merely decorative effect.

Though the curving plastic hose may have the most striking visual presence, the architects point out that 'all surfaces touched by the user are made of wood'. The hose structure, however, is key to other functions of the design apart from delivering solar-heated water. In some places it flattens out, presenting the greatest surface area to the sun. In another area it forms a screened changing space. The wooden structure supports the large expanse of hose, but also makes a shaded pergola, a deck area and a lounge chair. The contrasting properties of the two materials (plastic hose and wood planks), one being flexible and the other rigid, is celebrated by Müller and Quednau, who have taken full advantage of their complementary possibilities. The hose drapes and shades the wood structure in 'one

continuous sculpted ribbon', while also creating a seal, wedged in between the sections to make the tub watertight.

Originally sited in the gardens of the Schloß Solitude on the outskirts of Stuttgart as part of an exhibition, the Bad fitted in, say the architects, with the atmosphere of the former hunting grounds, which have become something of an 'outdoor fitness centre', attracting walkers, joggers and cyclists, and now a few hopeful bathers. The unit is mobile,

attaching to any nearby hydrant, though the water can take up to two hours to warm. Cold water can then be added to the bath by separate jets. After the tub is filled and the bather has enjoyed his or her outdoor bath, water can be released via hoses onto the ground.

Because of the way the city is fragmented, Müller and Quednau say that the landscape of the Schloß Solitude has become part of the urban infrastructure. So the elements of this project – the shape of the hoses, the contrast of materials – are also representative of the weaving of functional and leisure facilities in such an urban agglomeration. The fragmentation of the city has earned it the nickname of 'the German Los Angeles', a moniker that says a lot about contrasts and flexible thinking.

[left and below] When sealed between the wood slats, the one thousand metres of hose used to fill the bath also creates the bath structure. The wrapped hose works to shade the changing space.

Manual

① changing

② cleaning

BAD

③ filling   ④ draining

⑤ irrigating

[above] The water in the hose is warmed by the sun, a process which can take up to two hours. Cold water can then be added. After each bath, the water is released to irrigate the surrounding lawn.

modern love
La Estancia Chapel
Cuernavaca, Mexico
Bunker Arquitectura

The 2007 commission was to build a wedding chapel in a garden that is a popular venue for nuptial celebrations. The garden is located in Cuernavaca, the 'city of eternal spring', which sits in the Sierra Madre mountains and is dominated both by its ancient heritage and the Colonial style imposed by Spanish invaders in the 17th century. As ceremonies were previously conducted in the open air under a light canvas canopy roof, the brief was to build an 'open chapel' that reflected the city's Colonial tradition.

Esteban Suárez, Jorge Arteaga and Sebastian Suárez, principals of Bunker Arquitectura, proposed a different style, however, a radical departure from historic precedent. What they wanted to construct was, in effect, a modern glass box. The clients, say the architects, were 'violently opposed' to the idea of a glass chapel because of the potential 'greenhouse effect', which would make the space far too hot in the summer. But they relented, somewhat grudgingly, when the architects explained that by using a series of glass panels, or slats, they could create a sheltered, translucent space that would be easily cooled by cross-ventilation. The clients were also convinced by the argument that the contrast of the building with its surroundings would make it a unique, sculptural addition to the verdant setting.

And it is all that. It is also a structure of fine detail. Opaque U-glass reduces glare, and the lattice-type arrangement of slats spaced 10cm apart lets the breeze and the greenery flow around and through the space. By starting with a box shape and then compressing it slightly, the architects created a peaked roof, rather than the flat one of a perfect cube. Looking at the side walls, the oblique angle at the roofline is mirrored in the dip of glass panes along the base, making the conceit of compressing the box (and simultaneously pushing the ceiling line up and the floorline down) visible. Tiny floor lights embedded in the surrounding slab enhance the night-time magic of the low-lit crystalline structure.

The chapel is a work of sparkling individuality and bold modernity that, even without its religious designation, stands out as a piece of pure beauty. Celebrating the tropical surroundings, rather than thrusting the bulk and ornamentation of the Colonial style upon them, the architects have produced more than a fanciful wedding pavilion or a slice of wedding-cake architecture. Instead of looking to the past, the chapel is, rather appropriately and materially, a celebration of the present, and the future.

'The exuberant vegetation and tall jacaranda trees permeate the glass lattice walls, creating a graceful and rhythmic dialogue between the interior and exterior spaces.'

[above] The walls were made using 130 glass panels of varying lengths that are 7mm-thick and made from U-glass, which is often used as a double membrane to increase solar gains and insulating effects. Here, the single membrane creates a lattice effect that allows natural light and fresh air to flow through the structure, while the roof and foliage protect the building from the most direct sunlight.

La Estancia Chapel

curving craft
Jelly Architecture
Izu, Japan
Gin Johannes

The name sounds very whimsical, and Japanese architect Gin Johannes discusses his work with an almost child-like exuberance. He has described a similar project, his elevated walkway, as being 'like a ballet walk or Buto dancing spirit'. Many of his forms are dream-like, or look to be inspired by fantasy. In this 2005 project there seem to be some recognizable elements, but his re-casting of a shed in the garden next to his live/work space on the Izu peninsula is nothing to do with jellyfish and everything to do with his ambitions to manipulate lines into surprising shapes ('surface bending'), and then construct those shapes in real scale. It is also a result of his interest in new materials and in creating a structural skin that is translucent, transparent, and has the potential of fabric for being stretched taut, twisted and illuminated.

Computer software has been blamed for making it too easy for architects to indulge their own whimsy while creating things that are structurally impossible to build. But Johannes was eagerly exploring the possibilities of form well before the use of computer design tools became commonplace. As a student and for his first, award-winning designs, Johannes spent countless hours draughting his shapes by hand, but he has since happily embraced the new software, which he employs alongside his hand-drawn

sketches. Since he has built his designs, including Jelly Architecture, by hand, Johannes has little worry for whether the tools that get him to the final structure are hardware or software.

Being able to realize the forms himself makes Johannes more of a craftsman than his designs would immediately suggest. The steel-rod construction was first explored in his competition-winning 'Masques of the City' for the Brooklyn Heights Promenade. For the Jelly building, he welded and bent the steel rods himself and specified the fabric – translucent PVC sheets, with double-layer sections that he filled with a fluorescent-pink 'jelly' material. Sunlight through the pink 'window' casts a tinted glow in the interior. He also devised a special rubber joint to connect the sheets to the steel rods.

'Jelly architecture' describes both the loosely flowing structure and the bright-pink material Johannes has packed inside. But it also connotes something amorphous and changing, which belies the deliberate, closely monitored work of the architect here. Sometimes the best skill a craftsman can exhibit is that of making difficult tasks look easy. Johannes makes complicated forms that look much more naïve than they really are, but that are also probably as fun to inhabit as you might imagine.

'My opinion is that
architecture needs
a human scale, a
human-body sequence
and emotion.'

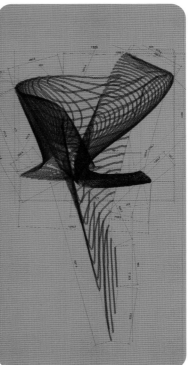

To create his 'jelly architecture', Johannes has been experimenting with form and materials for many years. Here, he has used 12mm-diameter rods, bent and welded by hand, as well as a custom rubber joint of his own invention for attaching the specially developed membrane which is stretched over the metal frame.

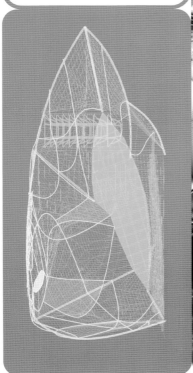

one man's rubbish

Crisp-Packet Shelter
Kent, England
Jack Woolley

This kind of resourcefulness used to be the domain of scouts and survivalists, finding a material that exists scattered around the local environment in abundance and using it to construct a weatherproof, easily portable shelter. But this is not a forest camp-out or a jungle training exercise, and such efficient shelters are not just for playthings or hobbies. Inspired 'by the natural disasters in 2005 that left many thousands of people homeless' and by the need to provide shelter quickly after such disasters as the Pakistan earthquake, which left rescue workers scrambling to bring in aid before the onset of winter, architect Jack Woolley started casting about for solutions. What he found was literally under his nose, at his feet, in fact, almost everywhere he looked.

It was around the major transportation hub of King's Cross station in central London that Woolley found his ideal material. There, he says, 'I took a wheelbarrow and collected six hundred discarded crisp packets, some recently thrown away, others much older.' After splitting them open and washing them, he discovered that even the older packets retained their shiny, reflective surface. This would be useful as it could reflect the sun or help retain heat, depending on which side of the packet was turned outwards. Looking closely at the composition of the material revealed two other important details: the laminate of polypropylene and foil used to resist moisture and keep crisps 'crisp' is impermeable, very effective for a shelter, and it is also very difficult to break apart and recycle. This makes a compelling argument for the reuse of this specially developed material. So compelling that after seeing his project, Walkers, a major manufacturer of crisps in the UK, began investigating the feasibility of using off-cuts from their packaging to construct such shelters.

The assembly demanded yet more scavenging and experimenting. Woolley explored a range of techniques for joining the washed and carefully opened packets: heat welding produced the strongest seam, so that was the method used to create one 6m x 3m sheet. The framework also needed to be easily 'found' since, as Woolley was well aware, the UN has experienced problems when essential components of their own emergency shelter kits, such as aluminium poles, were stolen and sold on the black market. Woolley's frame, therefore, was made of found copper plumbing pipes, 'soldered into a random collection of useful lengths', and then assembled into a rigid frame, onto which the patchwork sheet was wrapped around. The result may not be beautiful to look at, but it is a beauty of ingenuity and reuse, and makes a rather startling point about the urgent needs of some as measured against overabundance for others.

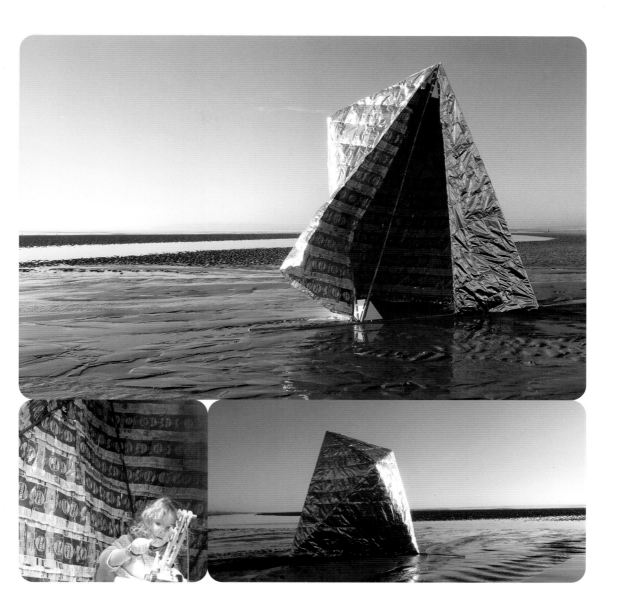

climate change
Glass Bubble
Malmö, Sweden
Monika Gora

Landscape architect and artist Monika Gora opened her own studio in 1989, successfully developing her skills both as a landscape and product designer. In recent years, she has turned to larger built projects that demonstrate her affinity for sculptural forms. Two Piers 2004, at Sidensjö in the north of Sweden, is a pair of minimal walkways that project out from a hillside towards a nearby lake, giving a feeling of suspension into the air space beyond the hill. The piers are particularly affecting when the hills are blanketed with snow.

The Glass Bubble, designed in 2006, is another project that combines the creation of a remarkable structure with a new appreciation of the landscape. Sited on the storm-swept shore of the Öresund, where winds and saltwater assault the hardiest of plants, the Bubble maintains a temperate microclimate in a fully transparent enclosure. The site was a nondescript patch of hardscape situated between mid-rise buildings and offered nothing more than a windswept passage from the city to the sea walk.

The elegant glass ovoid is now planted with exotic and rare species of flowering plants and fruit trees that offer a glimpse of more temperate climes. Bold colours and unusual lush foliage are visible from all angles outside clear, fine, untinted glass. Inside, the sound of running water and the balmy atmosphere of tropical vegetation create not only a

pleasant place to shelter, but a comfortable, verdant place from which to view the less hospitable, though still starkly beautiful, surroundings outside.

While greenhouses filled with tropical plants are not a revolutionary idea, especially in colder climates, the desire to create a fully glazed structure of the height and shape that Gora desired in such a thin layer of structural glazing represented a particular technical challenge. The softly curved form was created using complex geometry and

houses a volume of 890 cubic metres within a structure of steel framework and load-bearing glass. The final sculptural design was realized with the help of Delft engineers Octatube. According to Gora, even making a rendering of the shape required 'a new form of 3D drawing' that was more accurate than existing programs, so this software had to be developed. Only when that was achieved could the task of choosing, and in some cases creating, materials and construction hardware begin.

The flat panels used on the outside surface were selected in favour of warm, bent-glass panels for cost reasons. But other alternatives were considered and discarded because of their inability to meet the demands of the unusual shape and structure: cold, twisted panels were ruled out as their surface shape is difficult to control. The panels that were eventually chosen are made from low-iron glass for the greatest transparency and to reduce any greenish tint. The result is a structure of icy clarity.

[opposite] The structure is clamped together using laser-cut stainless-steel plates, with plastic spacers between the panels to help stiffen the surface and transmit forces from one panel to the next across the entire shell. The steel support structure was manufactured off-site in Delft, as the very minimal tolerance required a precision only achievable in factory conditions.

'The only thing that separates the luxuriant flowering garden inside and the stormy, exposed conditions outside is a wall of thin glass.'

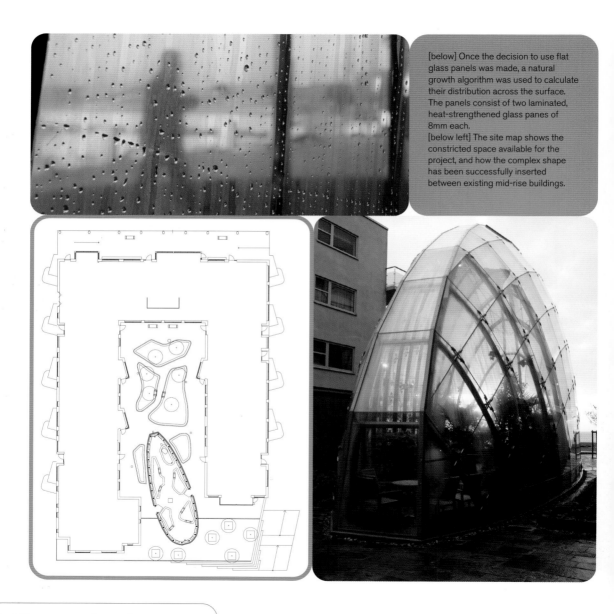

[below] Once the decision to use flat glass panels was made, a natural growth algorithm was used to calculate their distribution across the surface. The panels consist of two laminated, heat-strengthened glass panes of 8mm each.

[below left] The site map shows the constricted space available for the project, and how the complex shape has been successfully inserted between existing mid-rise buildings.

breathing freely

Tea House
Frankfurt, Germany
Kengo Kuma

Kengo Kuma is an architect known for his poetic structures in wood. These buildings often achieve a floating or ethereal quality because of their layered rows of slats with light flowing in and around them, so that they appear more like ribbons than structural framework. His Great (Bamboo) Wall house, among several earlier museums and domestic buildings, helped to crown him as something of a master of wood. But Kuma has achieved a similar effect in steel, glass, and even concrete, demonstrating that such rhythmic qualities could be created with a range of different materials used with a similar lightness of touch, attention to surface texture, and manipulation of natural light.

The Tea House was designed in 2007 for the garden of the Museum für Angewandte Kunst, which has an important collection of Japanese art from the Edo period. Kuma chose to create a 'breathing' architecture, rather than calling on a traditional or, as he calls it, 'defeated' architecture. 'To breathe', he explains, 'is to have an interactive communication between the environments.' The breathing conceit is literal as well as metaphorical: the diaphanous quality of the material allows movement and the structure is created by being filled with air.

The double-layer membrane is Tenara, a material that does not use glass fibres as a base and, according to the

architect, is therefore soft and light. Air flows between the two layers, which are attached using polyester string at a 600mm pitch, an arrangement that creates the dimpled effect that makes the otherwise marshmallowy form resemble a couple of golf balls melted together. Kuma's love of pattern is also recognizable here. The material is highly transparent, allowing for that interplay between the structure and its environment that the architect felt was key to the project.

Once again, Kuma shows that beauty is not only in the fabric of the building, but in the way it is worked in the design. It is a seemingly obvious notion, and yet we know all too well that one can make bad architecture with the best materials and beautiful buildings using only scrap. Here, a new and unusual skin has been made more extraordinary by the soft shape that sits in placid agreement with its garden setting. For those who would balk at the use of such an ephemeral structure for the age-old ceremony, it achieves its own poetic justice, since, as the architect points out, the Tea House 'originally came from a temporary space called a kakoi'. So the temporary nature of the inflatable house has a historic precedent, and the 'breathing' structure inspires something like a yogic meditation unifying body, mind and material.

'At times the architecture becomes small as it holds its breath, and at other times it breathes in deeply to become grander.'

The seafront along the west coast of England is known for its cold temperatures and high winds. The resort town of Blackpool is no exception, and also suffers from a traditional association with garish amusement halls, tacky souvenir shops and roaming packs of binge drinkers. At the turn of this century, city planners began an ambitious effort to rebrand the town to attract more discerning visitors. The plan to redevelop a section of the seaside promenade included seating, public art and a competition to design a series of rather sophisticated wind shelters.

The brief, according to competition-winning architect Ian McChesney, was pretty specific. It called for 'a rotating shelter, driven by a vane pointing into the prevailing wind and providing constant protection from the elements'. McChesney's immediate response was to combine the two functions – weathervane and shelter – into a single structure. He explains that he 'literally tore off a bit of paper and thought that surely, if it were just to twist, it would have the vane and the shelter'. Of course, he adds, 'I did that thing of trying out hundreds of other ideas, but I came back to my initial response.' Such a basic explanation belies the more complicated experiments with shape and wind speed, and the arrangement of the rotating mechanism that sits below ground and must periodically be cleaned as sand invariably gets in.

The 8m-tall structure is made of a special grade of stainless steel that is particularly resistant to corrosion, an essential consideration in the harsh environment where salt and sand make a continual assault on any surface. At the base, steel supports cantilever to hold a bench made of varnished oak. The wood was chosen because it was feared that steel would distort when welded and upset the balance of the structure. The varnish keeps it free from graffiti. The floor surface is a resin-bonded aggregate called Addagrip, lighter than standard Tarmac which would have been too weighty for the turntable mechanism below ground.

Wind speed had to be calculated over a number of conditions, not only to see whether the vane would turn enough, but to ensure that it wouldn't move too quickly for people to access it. For this reason, the architects installed a damper system below, 'a drum of oil with a paddle inside'. The sculptural dynamism of the three wind vanes along the south shore, in conjunction with the lighting and seating elements, is making a difference to this stretch of seafront. It's not quite the Riviera yet, but Blackpool has achieved something almost as remarkable in view of its popular image: a place for quiet repose.

'I made up hundreds of models, all of which were
slightly different – it became a bit of an obsession.'

[above and right] A rotating mechanism located below ground ensures that both the structure and its disk-shaped floor section turn smoothly as the wind blows. A damper mechanism keeps them from turning too quickly.
[opposite] A special grade of stainless steel was used for the structure which would be more resistant to corrosion in the salty air of the seaside.

Wind Shelter

art and craft

When structures becomes sculpture

It's become something of a cliché to talk about the question of whether architecture can be considered art. But, as in many areas, clichés don't always mean irrelevance. Architecture that aspires to, or is inspired by, sculptural forms can give us some of the most positive experiences of our built environment. Shapes that suggest motion or flight, organic blobs or strict geometries, those that have an immediately tactile appeal and others that create or skew perspectives are all going beyond function to establish a strong, visual presence. Whether the aim is to become an object of beauty, or to encourage us to adjust our perception of structure, the architect is making form at least as important as any practical use for which the building was conceived.

In some ways, the buildings in this chapter are at the extreme end of the spectrum. These are shapes that draw attention as sculpture so that their architecture may seem a secondary concern, though in most cases here, it is integral. In the metallic exuberance of Oyler Wu's Density Fields, the angular play of unit-design's Weather Tower and the smooth curves of Charlie Whinney's Rolling Summer House, a gauntlet seems to have been thrown down to colleagues and other builders to see art as a legitimate influence on structure and an imperative to embrace the creative exigencies of human activity.

The Windshape pavilion by nArchitects is a paean to both art and nature, with its delicate structure that moves with the wind but also creates a semi-enclosed rooftop seating and viewing area over the landscape below. Moving with the wind, too, is the prairie-inspired Mobile Chaplet by Moorhead & Moorhead, which successfully articulates references to pioneers, the Great Plains and cathedrals, while providing an inspired venue for contemplation.

Another kind of contemplation inspired French architect Philippe Rahm's design for House Dilation. With an infinitely expanding view, the structure can defy imposed barriers of structure and open our perspective, even our minds, to the world beyond four walls. Michael Jantzen's work is also about taking down walls, or taking down parts of walls and making them windows, and making windows into doorways. His M-Velope Two is a fascinating study in open and enclosed space and all of the permutations in between that make people feel adequately exposed or sheltered in their chosen place of reflection.

The selection in this chapter has a significant contribution from China, in the range of structures built for the Jinhua Architecture Park. Architects both new and notable designed pavilions for the park, which was completed in late 2007 as part of a new town development. The project was headed by artist and designer Ai Wei Wei, who initially consulted with Herzog & de Meuron on the overall plan. Their Reading Space uses local materials and finishes in a bold, organic form that creates a piece of landscape sculpture and a warren of tiny reading nests. Already making their presence known with the design for Beijing's 'Bird's Nest', Herzog & de Meuron, along with fellow Swiss architects Christ & Gantenbein and Fernando Romero from Mexico, were among several contributors from Europe and North America. Chinese architect Liu Jiakun also came up with a new approach to the traditional tea house by elevating it, literally, so that the view out becomes as important as the ceremony within.

exuberant tension

Density Fields
Los Angeles, California, USA
Oyler Wu Collaborative

Designing for an exhibition offers a prime opportunity for architects to flex their creative muscles. But as all projects have their constraints, so too do areas given over to architectural display. The outdoor exhibition space at Materials & Application, a centre in Los Angeles 'dedicated to pushing new and underused ideas in art, architecture and landscape into view', is just a small, gravel-laid courtyard on a busy street. This, however, proved all the more inspiring for architects Dwayne Oyler and Jenny Wu, who configured a structure in 2007 that is rooted in the confines of the proscribed space, but reaches out both visually and theoretically, well beyond its boundaries.

Oyler and Wu worked up their complex sculptural form by creating a number of 'exuberant models that extend lines from major points throughout the neighbourhood, including building openings, doors, windows and rooflines'. Following these 'imaginary sightlines', they then settled on a structure framed with aluminium tubes and strung with lengths of polypropylene rope. This 'extreme cantilever' is a three-dimensional expression of the lines mapped out in those models, an abstract shape founded on physical reference points. This is not an organic starburst, however, or a series of straight lines that radiate from a central point. There is much more complexity and richness to the design.

The framework consists of a series of irregular angles, like wing joints that are not consistent but lean towards a single direction, giving a real sense of motion. The architects then almost reverse the sensation in their exploration of tensile properties, stretching the fine ropes in precise geometries that pull the framework back into itself, but only enough to make the tension more palpable. The architects say they wanted to address the question of how lines differ according to their structural (or material) properties. The result of the contrast between the rigid aluminium and the tensioned polypropylene is to give the effect that the structure is spring-loaded, ready to advance.

The pair, who both teach design studios at the Southern California Institute of Architecture, share a professed interest in exploiting 'the characteristics that are latent in every site'. Here, they have seemingly pulled something out of a hat, since the bland, semi-urban streetscape offers little in the way of features on which to hang a concept or design. But as if to prove that any patch of ground can become a launchpad for ideas, Density Fields references unseen ideas (a string instrument played by the wind) with the literally uplifting (one half of a lightweight aircraft) to not only break through boundaries, but to make the viewers forget they even exist.

'A series of fine, tensioned ropes pull the cantilever in the opposite direction, forcing it to hover above the ground.'

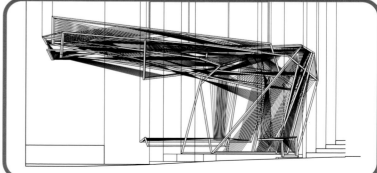

[below] In a neighbourhood dominated by hardscape and concrete boxes, the architects inserted a structure of visual delicacy. The 8m-long cantilever is tensioned with polypropylene ropes. Angles or projection were determined by sketching connections between the site and others in the area. The abstract form also includes 'furniture' elements, a table and bench.

favourable conditions

Weather Tower
Offenbach-am-Main, Germany
unit-design with Boris Banozic

As architecture parks go, this could certainly mark the emergence of a new trend. Having been asked to come up with an idea for a new public space, the Frankfurt-based group unit-design hit on the theme of weather-watching. Located in an area of relatively flat landscape and wide vistas, the city of Offenbach-am-Main provided suitable ground for observing any weather conditions that might be looming in the distance or racing across the horizon.

In developing the 'weather park', unit-design, with director Bernd Hilpert and colleague Peter Eckart, led a group of designers to create exhibits and editorial information that would help visitors to understand the patterns and movement of weather in the region. While several designers went to work experimenting with everything from sculptural windsocks to rain shelters, the unit-design team decided to put visitors where the action was, at the top of a tower with views in all directions. But the structure does more than lift people up and show them the view; it combines the references and tools of meteorology with abstract sculptural form.

The weather tower is a slightly off-kilter, three-legged construction that seems to lean on a fourth support, a steeply ascending metal stair. According to architect Boris Banozic, the design was inspired by weather instruments balanced on a tripod, so that it 'symbolizes the function of observing and analyzing'. The observation deck stands on the three steel columns, which are made more visible by red and white swirls that give the impression of a construction zone. Additional support is provided by the double-flight steel staircase and braced handrail. The platform is 10m above ground level and, in clear conditions, visitors can obtain a view over thirty kilometres.

The sculptural interpretation of meteorological instruments continues at the top of the platform with a new take on the traditional 'ocular', an element that points the viewer towards significant landmarks. Here it has been recast as a 'directional loop', an open rectangular ribbon of steel. Schematic charts on the railing help to inform visitors about impending weather conditions, using aspects of the view and visibility to explain atmospheric opacity and the approach of weather fronts. But the angular metal shape also acts as an open-air picture frame, holding the outspread landscape within its limits. It is pointed in the direction of Frankfurt, and natural and man-made landmarks, such as the Taunus mountains and city skyscrapers, are used for reference on the information panels.

Though it is perfectly sturdy and well placed, the structure is deliberately insubstantial, with spindly legs

appearing liable to tip at a strong gust. Perhaps it is part of the experience of weather, a tool that raises visitors up to a clear view while still allowing them to feel vulnerable to the natural roil of the atmosphere.

'By observing the degree of haze and looking at the schematic weather charts on the railing, the visitor is informed of upcoming weather situations.'

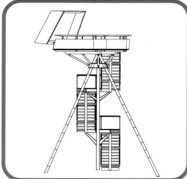

[left and right] The observation platform can accommodate ten to fifteen people. The 'directional loop' points the view towards Frankfurt, but the expanse of flat landscape allows for a generous view of incoming weather.
[below] The tower is a sculptural intersection of lines and rectilinear volumes.

adding on
House Dilation
Cumbria, England
Philippe Rahm

The inspiration came from the writer Georges Perec, who is said to have expressed the dream of having a house in Paris with 'his living room in the Latin Quarter, his study close to the Champs-Élysées, his bedroom in Montmartre and his bathroom on the Île de la Cité'. According to avant-garde architect Philippe Rahm, this idea was not formed out of a love of the City of Lights, or a desire to be everywhere in it at once, but by the fact that different rooms which harbour distinct activities benefit from separate locations due to climatic reasons, such as the fall and flow of natural light, and purpose. Rahm's solution is to separate rooms completely and place them in their appropriate setting, even if that places the bathroom hundreds of metres or a kilometre away from the bedroom, and the living room in an altogether different setting. The reasoning, according to Rahm, is the same that determines which streetside café we choose to sit at: the particular time of day, the degree of sunlight and warmth, activity, view. So while the overall effect is that of a house, the architect and the user each concentrates on the single space.

This all has a rather Parisian ring to it, but Rahm has brought the idea to a more general conclusion. Rather than gathering together the rooms that make up the spaces of a house into a single block, they could be dispersed, with, say,

a bedroom located in the north, where there is less natural light, but overlooking some greenery, the living room in the south (or towards the afternoon sun), the kitchen in a spot of morning sun. Instead of thresholds between rooms that measure a few centimetres, they would dilate as far as necessary. Nothing is fixed, however, so the user could inhabit any room for any purpose at the desired moment of the day.

Rahm has not said much about power and services, but the plan isn't merely theoretical. He has been commissioned to produce House Dilation for Grizedale Arts in Cumbria, an organization that is part of the Land Art movement in the UK and promotes experimental contemporary art. There, he says, the house will be dilated across meadows, forests and fields, where the climatic qualities of light, temperature and humidity created by trees will influence the activity carried out in that particular 'dilation'. A repetitive structure of a rectangular steel frame and glass walls will be used to construct each of the separate elements. The ideal, from an efficiency point of view, would be if multiple users could inhabit the different rooms at the same time according to their particular needs as a sort of dilated community – rather like loaning out your Montmartre aerie while you take your favourite seat at Le Dôme.

'The house is no longer a compact and closed object; it bursts, disseminating its layout and its spaces in different locations over the site, multiplying the views, the situations, the sites, the atmospheres and the climates.'

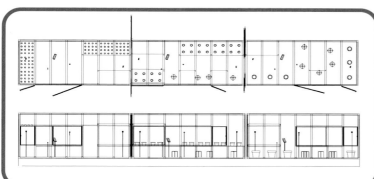

[left] The house adapts its plan
according to the external qualities of
the site. The surrounding environment
creates the purpose of each room.
[below and opposite] The seemingly
conceptual project will be realized in
the UK using rectangular steel frames
and glass walls.

round and round

Rolling Summer House
England
Charlie Whinney

After studying 3D Design for Sustainability at Falmouth College of Arts in Cornwall, Charlie Whinney began designing with the aim of creating sculptural works using local, unseasoned timber. The Rolling Summer House, one of his first large-scale designs, won immediate acclaim in a series of exhibitions across the UK in 2007.

The concept came out of a commission by a forest conservation charity to produce a centrepiece for a series of 'wood fairs' to promote locally sourced timber and demonstrate its potential as a building material. The brief also specified a structure that could be installed or removed in a matter of minutes, and that could be easily reproduced. Whinney's design is highly mobile, as it can be rolled into place, quite literally, and then fixed into position, even on a hill, using child-safe legs. It is self-contained with an enlarged entrance that also functions as a seat, and comes with its own trailer. But while issues of mobility were successfully addressed, the idea of reproducing more rolling pavilions belies the painstaking process by which this first form was achieved.

The project evolved from Whinney's experiments based on a 'grid-shell system', and is a dramatic example of the lengths to which the artist/designer will go 'to create seemingly impossible pieces of work out of solid timber'.

Inspired by the forms of microscopic plankton and seed heads, the form of the Rolling Summer House was designed by careful calculation using mathematical formulae linked to patterns in nature and the golden ratio. To achieve a range of shapes in furniture and outdoor sculpture, Whinney had, with his former collaborators, helped to develop unique methods and equipment for steaming and bending wood. In this case, he used his skill with an understanding of the material to utilize another aspect of its character: the tendency of wood to 'un-bend' in damp environments. This natural movement creates tension that is used to brace the large segments of oak and ash that make up the interior and exterior of the summer house, respectively. According to Whinney, this natural tension 'makes it stronger than it would otherwise have been'.

Like many garden or forest pavilions, the framed wood sphere inspires natural delight in its playful form and is very appealing to children. Once secured in place, it is robust enough to be climbed on and explored. Children can even run up and down the curved floor inside, while adults admire the combination of solidity and delicacy that make up the naturally inspired form.

[opposite] The tendency of wood to 'un-bend' in natural environments helps create the tension that stabilizes the form. The structure utilizes the double-layered 'grid-shell system' which the designer has been developing through a series of bent wood projects.

[right] The network of bentwood straps on the outer shell make an exceedingly strong, though visually delicate, support for the solid core.

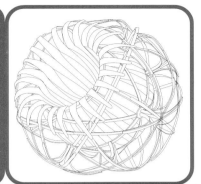

'[The house] has been likened to a giant piece of pollen.'

Rolling Summer House

far pavilions
Jinhua Architecture Park
Jinhua, China
Various

In 2002 the city of Jinhua, in the Zheijiang province of central China, decided to create a 'new district' out of former agricultural land to provide housing and services for the growing population. A 2km-long strip along the Yiwu River was set aside for a public park and museum, and the municipal government handed control of the design to famed artist Ai Wei Wei, the son of the well-known dissident poet, Ai Qing. Ai Wei Wei is himself a controversial though very popular figure, who has been openly critical of the Chinese government. His performance art, sculpture and photographic compositions make him among the most prominent figures of the Chinese avant garde, so it is perhaps surprising to learn that he has been involved in such major, state-supervised projects.

Ai Wei Wei envisioned an architecture park with designs submitted from both inside and outside China. The final seventeen pavilions, built by sixteen Chinese and international architects (including Herzog & de Meuron, whose recent projects include their stadium for the 2008 Beijing Olympic Games), were finished and the park opened in October 2007. Among the structures were a restaurant, coffee house, Internet café, multimedia space, 'book-bar', an 'archaeological archive' designed by Ai Wei Wei, and several less specifically functional follies. Styles range from traditional forms to sculptural to futuristic in a varied palette of materials.

While the land offered space for more buildings, the idea was to set each pavilion in a generous plot of open land, some of which have views of the river. The result is a microcosm of architecture from China to Europe, with projects being supervised from offices in Austria, the Netherlands, Switzerland, Germany, the United States and Mexico, over three years of construction. Some saw the collection of structures as a gesture in China's step towards international participation with the Beijing Olympics; others hoped the park's symbolic exchange of ideas would encourage further such interaction from both sides of the political and geographic borders. Although Ai Wei Wei would later denounce what he saw as China's unabashed propagandist approach to hosting the 2008 summer games, his efforts in bringing together such a wide-ranging collection of designs and practitioners will provide a tangible legacy of international cooperation.

Rather like very large birdhouses, Liu Jiakun's Tea Rooms perch delicately in the air to welcome guests, providing a rather spectacular view, a raised shelter, and perhaps other treats. Given a site on a spot of lowland, the architect decided to invite visitors up into his elevated boxes so that they could enjoy a view of the river, as well as a tea break.

Yet whatever quaint images one might conjure of the tea house typology are immediately dispelled by Liu Jiakun's bold choice of hard industrial materials. The main support is provided by electrical poles, which, as he says, 'can reach anywhere and so do these mini-structures'. Rather than traditional wood, other readily available robust materials, such as grilled steel, aluminium alloy and steel cable, are used to form the basic pavilion, while polycarbonate sheets take the place of rice-paper sliding doors.

Such a minimal design requires that some of the elements perform dual functions, but there is beauty in such efficiency. That the handrail actually doubles as a water pipe is a basic piece of building ingenuity, but no less remarkable for that. With their opening and closing panels and elevated viewpoints, the Tea Rooms maximize a small area of land by offering a variety of perspectives and spatial sensations. The materials may be of an industrial character, but the effect is to dignify them by design.

[left] At night, the lighted Tea Rooms appear like delicate paper lanterns set out in the landscape.
[below] Close up, the visitor appreciates the elegant utility of industrial materials.

'The mobility and little surprises in the design are meant to stimulate joyful experiences.'

Reading Space
Jinhua Architecture Park
Herzog & de Meuron

Probably the biggest star in the constellation of designers participating in the Jinhua project, Herzog & de Meuron had already established an identity in China with their design for the Beijing National Stadium, the centrepiece for the 2008 Olympic Games. As they had been working on a masterplan for the new city centre, the architects were asked by director Ai Wei Wei to help with the selection of projects for the park. Reading Space reflects the geometric patterning they have employed elsewhere in the centre, but on a minute scale. The idea was to not only repeat the pattern of the organizing principle, but to give it depth, so that the design 'overcomes its two-dimensionality' and 'becomes space in its own right'. While working in computer programs, the duo discovered their chosen form to be more difficult than they had anticipated, but also more productive, so that they ended up with three versions of the pavilion, one of which would be placed in Jinhua and the others used in Genoa and Basel.

Their final design for Jinhua was built in dyed concrete, and their difficult shape began to take form offering specific features such as seating areas, overhangs and small spaces for retreat, like in a window seat or a treehouse. The architects enjoyed the fact that these spaces were not deliberately demarcated, but follow naturally within the flow of the structure.

'The geometric pattern was meant to be more than a mere veil. It was meant to overcome its superficial two-dimensionality and generate a potential from which the whole world could be imagined and built — somewhat like a molecular structure or a genetic code.'

art and craft

The structure was made of dyed concrete using on-site formwork. To arrive at the final form, the architects began with a geometric pattern that they had used in a masterplan for a nearby city centre. To make the pattern more dynamic, it was projected into a cube using a computer program. The resulting virtual spatial grid rendered a form that offered such features as seating and reading spaces.

Reading Space

The Ancient Tree
Jinhua Architecture Park
Christ & Gantenbein

For the Swiss practice Christ & Gantenbein, the opportunity to design a pavilion for Jinhua's new architecture park was a chance to stand back and look again at the basics: 'The project, since it has not been assigned any specific function, is about creating a place in its most archaic notion: it offers shelter.' Inspired by 'the Chinese tradition of creating gardens filled with artificial lakes, mountains, stones, plants, animals', the architects decided to re-create a revered form, the ancient tree, as a place for shelter and reflection.

The choice of concrete and 'low-tech' construction methods was a reflection of the local building techniques, and gives the structure a strength and integrity similar to that inherent in giant trees. The pavilion is formed by a massive central stem, with a panel roof and twenty-four 'ribs' that protrude like branches and support the roof structure. Each of the ribs has been cast in-situ in forms that simulate a natural leafy outline. The rib elements hang lower on one side, giving the effect of a tree that has been bent by wind or old age. As they taper towards the 'trunk', the ribs produce a fluted central column that recalls the gnarled and veined surfaces of old trees. The concrete was also chosen for its natural weathering, but the grey hue and overhanging shapes also deliver a mystic, fairy-tale quality, or at least something that promises more than shade.

According to the architects, 'the whole production process is intended to take into account the local building conditions'. Construction is deliberately low-tech and adaptable. To avoid large-scale transport of prefabricated pieces, the branches, or 'ribs', were cast in-situ. These were hung one by one using metal rings. The roof elements could be prefabricated or cast on site and then pinned to the ribs.

'Being reminiscent of an ancient tree ... the structure is something between an archaic object and a technically rationalized piece of architecture.'

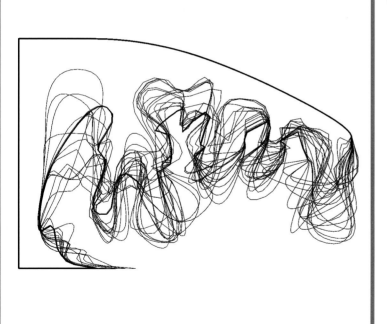

Bridging Tea House
Jinhua Architecture Park
Fernando Romero

On a site next to a pond, architect Fernando Romero devised
a sculptural addition to the Jinhua Architecture Park that
combines 'two fundamental elements of Chinese gardens:
the bridge and the tea house'. Drawing on the gardens'
repertoire of dynamic lines and angles, the team delivered a
'structural maze' in brightly painted concrete that spans the
pond, framing views through orthogonal openings. The aim
was to create individual 'cells', or 'micro-ambiences', within
the small space, so that each has its own 'accessibility,
identity and privacy', while also being open to the landscape.
This amounts to combining simplicity and complexity, creating
various divisions within a simple volume. The integrated stair
means that the interior is full of movement and shifting
perspectives interspersed with seating areas.

Working at such a great geographical distance was a
challenge. 'After sending our schematic design to the Chinese
organization, communication stopped,' Romero explains.
After a year, the organization 'sent an email with a picture of
an almost finished pavilion'. If it's a leap of faith that allowed
the architects involved to contribute such a bold flourish to
a newly created park space, it has been rewarded with a
landscape of extraordinary experiments in shape, perception
and materials, and a tremendous spirit of international
collaboration.

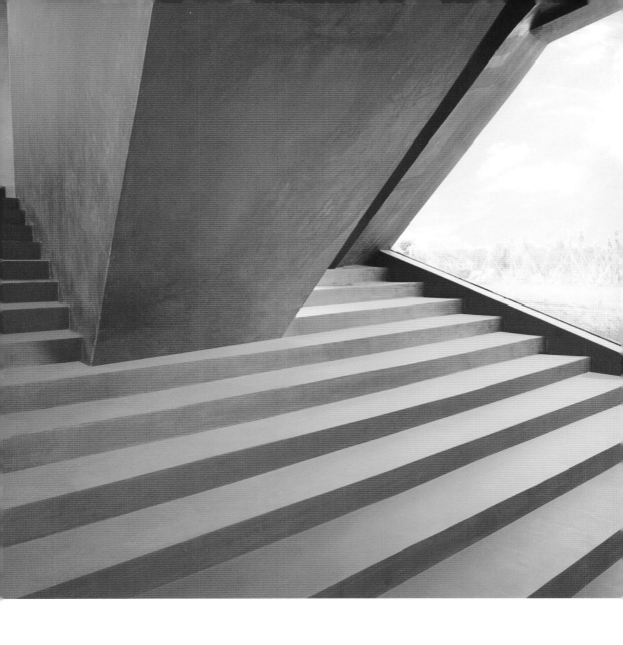

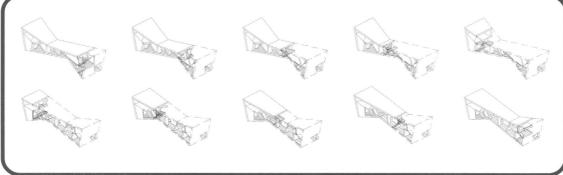

[above] The continuous stair combined with window openings of varying shapes creates a dynamic interior of shifting perspectives.
[opposite] Romero combined low-tech building materials (dyed concrete) with sharp modern geometries to create a fusion of the ornamental bridge and tea pavilion. The 'structural maze' spans the pond while allowing a variety of observation points.

'Being next to a pond, we wanted to unify both typologies – the bridge and the tea house – into one single structure.'

Designer and artist Michael Jantzen has made a career (and a long list of projects) from reordering planes like so much architectural origami. In his many designs for pavilions and open-air studios, he seems to start with the idea of boxes being opened in surprising ways. But the end result is never a box. Even when fully closed, his M-Velope and M-Velope Two (2007) are more a concatenation of geometric forms. In fact, Jantzen's preferred form for these structures is in their partially opened, slightly mixed-up state, when, as he sees it, there is some chaos in the geometry.

In his M-Velope series, Jantzen has taken the standard material of garden furniture — hardwood slats — and rearranged it into shifting planes and unusual angles so that the familiar gazebo becomes both a functional shelter and a far more intriguing piece of backyard sculpture. It is a restrained and highly civilized chaos, offering control of light and air by opening and closing panels to varying degrees as needed. Like many works of architecture/sculpture, it is both something to look at and something people want to be in and explore. What makes it more interesting for most visitors is the degree of interaction that it offers: not only opened or closed, but at so many stages in between.

The structure consists of a basic frame that is then hung with the slatted panels that have been subdivided in different ways. They can be simple rectangles or more irregular trapezoidal forms that fold in half by way of hinged joints. By opening, or partially opening, different panels, the interior can be more or less secluded/protected and open to sunlight, and then, of course, the form becomes more unusual. Benches and folding backrests are built into the internal framework. The frame is steel and wood (sustainably grown Western Red Cedar), which is painted or stained. A solar panel can be added to provide energy for lighting if desired.

Jantzen refers to these designs as 'functional art', and says that he created the M-Velopes as 'special places to meditate', but to give oneself over to meditation in such a structure means that somehow the constant urge to arrange and rearrange would have to be subdued and some amount of chaos allowed to stand.

meditation on wheels

Mobile Chaplet
Fargo, North Dakota, USA
Moorhead & Moorhead

Its shape, say the architects, was inspired by the forms of both the covered wagons used by new settlers to cross the country in the 19th-century and by vaulting church naves. Yet the sweeping linearity of the Mobile Chaplet also deftly mirrors the miles of prairie grass that used to spread out across these once-wild American plains. The design was created as part of the Roberts Street Chaplet Project, initiated by artist Marjorie Schlossmann, who purchased a small building in downtown Fargo, North Dakota, which she then renovated and filled with her own paintings. The project grew out of Schlossmann's desire to 'create more structures with the same purpose – sacred spaces, open to the public, open to people of all religious and secular belief systems, free of charge, and full of art'.

Architects Robert and Granger Moorhead are brothers who have their own architectural practice in New York, but hail from North Dakota, where their architect father, Richard, still practices. Consulting with their father on the entry for this travelling show of meditative spaces, the Moorhead brothers studied patterning and 'explored forms that could be created by weaving a series of rods of identical length'. The variation in height and shape comes from the fact that the rods are anchored at different points along the periphery of the structure. The final, undulating shape was

achieved by weaving together two vaulted forms, one inside the other, over and through the surrounding bench, which is in turn supported by the rods. The rods also make a backrest for the bench.

Altogether two hundred 9m-long thermoplastic composite rods are used to define a space that is 4m high, 2.5m wide and 5m deep. Sitting on a flatbed trailer in a grassy field, all of its references – the covered wagon, the church vaulting, the prairie grass – are clearly visible, a remarkable feat for such a slight and unimposing structure. Schlossmann's painting in this chaplet is on the floor. For all of its mechanical considerations, the chaplet almost dissolves against its natural background, the open weave joining it to the sweep of the landscape against the horizon. Or perhaps it is just that the covered wagon shape has become such a symbol of the Midwestern heritage that this skeletal version (made of high-tech plastic elements) seems uniquely at home in its setting.

The six portable structures of the Roberts Street Chaplet Project were first exhibited in July 2006 in the grounds of the North Dakota Museum of Art. From there they were moved to a mall car park in downtown Fargo.

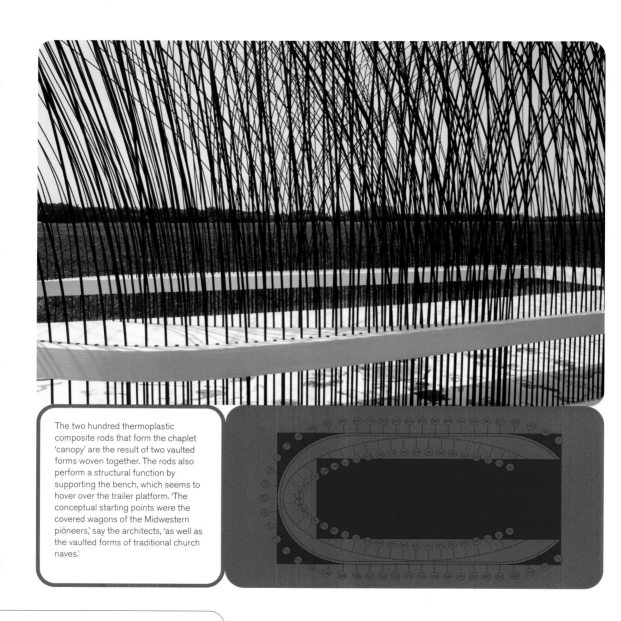

The two hundred thermoplastic composite rods that form the chaplet 'canopy' are the result of two vaulted forms woven together. The rods also perform a structural function by supporting the bench, which seems to hover over the trailer platform. 'The conceptual starting points were the covered wagons of the Midwestern pioneers,' say the architects, 'as well as the vaulted forms of traditional church naves.'

wind song

Windshape
Lacoste, France
nArchitects

In Provence, a land famed for its formidable Mistral, the prevailing building type is stone: hard, immovable, permanent. The cliff faces that tower over the valleys form jagged parades, as do the old houses. In the medieval village of Lacoste, the limestone walls and terraces form the backdrop for winding roads, terraced buildings and dramatic outcroppings, but so does the wispy greenery of vineyards, trees, fields, hanging bunches of growth and lavender bushes. As the strong winds make their way around the stone obstructions, they play through the soft vegetation, so that movement and the sound of leaves fluttering, branches swaying and creaking, is as much a part of the local atmosphere as the ancient stone. It was that effect of the wind on the 'luminous, soft, changeable landscape' that the architects sought to re-create with their cliffside pavilion.

The Windshape was meant to be a temporary structure, erected in 2006, and became a public meeting space, as well as a venue for concerts, exhibitions and ceremonies. The site, an exposed terrace jutting out from the hillside, provided the architects with the perfect opportunity (or, as they call it, 'laboratory') to experiment with building something that was not wind-proof, but rather wind reactive: 'It allowed us to test the idea of a building that can respond to natural stimuli.'

Using a system of plastic pipes threaded with polypropylene string that were joined and stretched by aluminium collars, they created two 8m-high pavilions that move and sound with the wind. By varying the degrees of tension in the string, and depending on the strength of the breeze, the movements go 'from rhythmic oscillations to ripples across the surface'. They can also billow in and out like puffed and slack sail cloth. The movement of the wind

through the strung shapes creates a range of sounds; in a particularly strong wind the noise can be very dramatic, say the architects, 'hissing like dozens of jump ropes'.

Visually, the Windshape is a delicate webbed crown sitting atop the hard stone. The tapering pipes echo the shapes of the fir trees that dot the landscape. The 'stacked and staggered tripods' that form the basic framework are softened with curved elements and arched openings where the strings were 'pinched' to one side. This framed design was meant to reflect the 'angular geometry' of the natural stone and built landscape, while also referring to the mutable natural growth. Hard and soft, dense and delicate, nature presents a rich palette of contrasts for the interested architect to learn from. The hums and sways of the Windshape communicate something of those riches to be discovered.

The larger pavilion is on a terrace next to the Porte du Garde, or main gate of the fortifications. The architects explain: 'We imagined that there might have been a tower there, and produced a sort of fictional reconstruction.'

'The project shows that architecture can respond to the elements in beautiful ways, connecting its inhabitants to a dynamic environment.'

scenic routes

Huts, pods and lookouts in remote landscapes

'The largest wilderness looks larger seen through a window,' as writer G.K. Chesterton observed, and sometimes it takes a well-placed window to help us appreciate what is beyond it. It is the two extremes of this perspective — the vast open landscape and the small building — that are the focus of this chapter. There are a number of reasons why a miniature structure surrounded by open space and natural beauty is so alluring. Perhaps the most obvious is that the sweeping vistas make us (and our constructions) feel less significant, opening up the world beyond. The thing that wants to be small and doesn't propose to contend with nature, but to become lost or hidden within it, speaks to our desire to be folded into that landscape ourselves, harking back to a childhood memory of hiding in trees.

But perching in trees is as much about the view as it is about the camouflage. Rural Studio's Bird Tower does not make the claim of being a new building, but is rather a reclaimed fire tower in the hardwood forest of the southeastern United States. The disused structure is now a popular venue for spotting rare species whose protection, by that very paradox of modern preservation, may be dependent upon human intervention. Another intervention, a viewing platform by Robbrecht & Daem, is a small gesture, but if it encourages people to see the surrounding landscape as something worth preserving, then its impact will be in inverse proportion to its size. A more dramatic viewing structure is the Aurland Lookout, perched high up above a glacial lake in Norway. As graceful and beautiful as it is, it relies on the awesome panorama of snow-covered mountains and forest to imbue its gentle curves with greatness. Similarly, Rodrigo Sheward's Observation Deck overlooking an active volcano is an elegant structure that epitomizes what surrounds it.

The extreme aspect of some of these projects has to do with how little they consume from the landscape. Casey Brown's Permanent Camping provides the necessary comforts, but demands little of its site and can resist the elements without protective finishes or barriers. The transportable Rolling Huts likewise encourage a sense of community while also being mindful of their physical footprint. Community is part of the inspiration for Dré Wapenaar's sculptural tent frames. His dual aims of being kind to the environment while encouraging social interaction derive from nomadic practices, but his approach and low material demands are enabled by modern means.

Tents and mobile structures have in common a subservience to the climate and the terrain, using minimal material to give access to the natural environment and not demanding a permanent place. Some projects have made a virtue of almost disappearing into the landscape. Among these, Snøhetta's Eggum Tourist Point is particularly successful in providing elegant functional space while almost withdrawing from view. Drawn up against a sharp cliffside, Hérault Arnod's Information Point reconciles the earlier intrusions of industry to the area, embedding those references into their design.

Finally, one project appears like a little celebration of local climate and culture. Sami Rintala's Floating Sauna is a very simple design for a structure that has a long and potent history in Scandinavian culture. Designed to float onto the fjord during cold weather without mechanical noise or pollutants, it seems an apt symbol for how humans can create a comfortable small presence in areas of extreme natural beauty.

far out

Aurland Lookout
Aurland, Norway
Saunders & Wilhelmsen

It projects and bends over the cliff face like a flexed limb, with all the grace and poise of a diver about to spring into flight over the fjord below. This 2005 project came out of a competition held by the Norwegian Highways Department to create a lookout point for a site of extreme natural beauty. And it is not difficult to imagine how the judges were attracted by the smooth elegance of the design and the minimal intrusion on the landscape. The architects wanted to enhance the drama of the setting by 'creating the experience of leaving the mountainside', as if stepping out into space. They also wanted to make it possible for visitors to behold the natural surroundings from a different standpoint.

Such ambitions seem simple enough to apprehend, but achieving them meant creating a car park farther away from the site, since in high season tour buses and cars fill the roads as visitors from all over the world come to take in the spectacular views of the mountains and fjords. The structure is like a bridge that has been stopped short of the opposite bank, so that it hangs as if in mid-air. In reality, there is a glass barrier at the far, projecting end, and the wooden horizontal curves down to join with a steel frame that has been anchored to the cliff below. The bridge joins a path at the side of the road and passes near the tops of the preserved pine trees and extends some 20m beyond the

hillside. As the architects put it, people can 'walk out into the air through the treetops'.

Todd Saunders and Tommie Wilhelmsen were always driven by their concern for preserving the natural environment as much as possible, while also helping visitors to experience the grandeur of the setting for themselves. They have created an inspiring structure that does just that. While wood construction is an obvious choice for such a setting, their particular treatment of the material as a multi-

layered, streamlined shape makes it a pleasing, sculptural presence that even with its dramatic projection from the cliff does not diminish the impact of the background. Also remarkable is that despite the large tourist numbers, the shape and daring site of the lookout allow visitors to feel some amount of solitude against and within this stunning panorama.

[above] The smooth wood surface contrasts with the icy jagged peaks in winter, but the streamlined shape is in keeping with the sheer drops of the granite cliffs. From a distance, it appears to be some kind of extreme diving platform.
[right] The drawing reveals the dramatic angle of the cliffside structure.

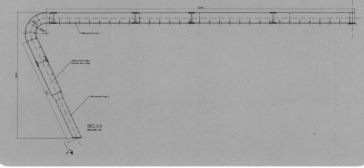

[below] The viewing platform strikes out in a sharp perpendicular to the cliff face. The angled supporting member and glazed barrier are not immediately visible from above, giving the bracing impression [right] of a clear drop at the end of the walkway.

'We called our competition entry "640m
over Aurland and 20,120km from Tokyo",
keeping in mind the uniqueness of the
place and the bigger picture.'

a raised outlook

Boston Pendulum
Boston, Lincolnshire, England
Robbrecht & Daem

It isn't the most remote location. The surrounding natural landscape is not the most dramatic. But a pair of viewing towers – one in Boston (the Boston Pendulum) and the other in Lincoln (the Lincoln Stump, a reference to the 'Boston Stump', or more formally St Botolph's, the tallest church tower in England) – created by Belgian architects Robbrecht & Daem to sit along the River Witham, make an exceptional experience in the landscape.

The towers came about as part of a competition held by the sustainable transport charity, Sustrans, to mark the beginning and end of a cycle path that runs 55km from the town of Boston to Lincoln. The path is part of the National Cycle Network which currently consists of over 19,000km of cycle and walking routes throughout the UK. In addition to promoting travel by cycle in a traffic-free location, the Boston Pendulum offers a rare chance in this flat landscape for elevated views over the countryside and opportunities for birdwatchers to observe species native to the fens. The two towers have also become popular viewing platforms for the annual Boston Rowing Marathon, a 50km race that takes place in September.

Robbrecht & Daem are a well-established practice with plenty of private and commercial commissions, such as banks and the Bruges Concert Hall, in their portfolio. But they also enjoy working on smaller, more artistic projects. Their approach to the Boston Pendulum is to make a piece of architecture with simple demands that still has some subtle complexity about it. The angular shape with its viewing platform that juts out 5m above the cycle path both engages with the users of the path and retreats into the greenery alongside. The steel-frame structure is softened with a palisade of larch that screens the frame and adds colour (being painted red and blue in a pattern conceived according to Robbrecht's own personal numerical system). As you ascend the tower, the screen to one side is higher; as you turn to ascend the next flight of stairs, the asymmetry shifts so that another view/enclosure perspective is offered.

The tower offers what Paul Robbrecht describes as painterly views over the land, which he feels could inspire people to see and better appreciate the setting that surrounds them. It may not compete with the 83m tower of the Boston Stump, but Robbrecht & Daem's structure has added another perspective on the fens, one that is more geared towards those with their feet on the ground.

arctic rest stop

Eggum Tourist Point
Lofoten, Norway
Snøhetta Architects

Located well within the Arctic Circle (at around the 67th Parallel), Lofoten is a western archipelago of Norway and a popular tourist destination. Increasing tourist numbers, with the addition of the E10 route in 1992, called for a reorganization of this popular point on Norway's west coast, facing the North Sea. Visitors come for snorkelling, even surfing, but mostly for the dramatic landscape that includes mountains formed from the oldest rocks on Earth, some three billion years old, and others that were revealed only in the last Ice Age, a mere ten thousand years ago. Lofoten is also known for its wildlife: Arctic species, including puffins, seals and orcas, are often on view, while many others pass by in their migration southward.

The site for new tourist facilities was an existing mound, Kvalhausen, which had been part of a small quarry and was used during the Second World War by German troops who had built a fortification on top that enclosed a radar station. The mound was also used as a lookout point to the North Sea, and marks a path to a nearby rock believed to have been used for sacred offerings during the Stone Age.

So the task of creating a rest stop for buses, cars, caravans, cyclists and walkers was as much about preserving the views and dramatic natural landscape as it was about adding shelter and services. The Norwegian firm of Snøhetta, recently lauded for their Oslo Opera House, were chosen for a design, realized in 2007, that enhances the existing conditions using natural materials and fitting as smoothly as possible into the terrain.

The main project involved creating a service building with an 'amphitheatre' that would provide some space for parking. Outside this area, additional space was allocated for camper vans. The contours of the mound and hillside have been preserved, as has the wartime fortification. A previous excavation in the mound was used as a starting point for service rooms, which include a multi-purpose room with a small kitchen and toilet facilities. From inside the tight dug-out space, a neat concrete box anchors an additional, slightly narrower, box structure that projects from the hill and is clad in planed local driftwood. The integrity of the landforms was secured with the addition of stone gabions that also make up seating and stepped access to the mound. Those stacked cages of rock are tied to the landscape visually and substantively, as the morainic stone came from the recent excavation and match that of the military fortification.

[above] Gravel and sand were
separated out and used as backfill.
The wooden volume is clad inside and
out with thick planking of driftwood
gathered from the beach, a few
hundred metres from the building.
[opposite] An existing fortification from
the Second World War was retained.
The new block utilizes a space
previously dug from the ancient
mounds, which has been reinforced
with stone gabions.

'The mound was once used as a collective local
lookout point for wives awaiting their husbands'
return from the sea.'

new village people

Tent Village Revisited
Nantes, France
Dré Wapenaar

It is safe to say that Dré Wapenaar is an expert on tents. He has made tents for single people, families, even a small, tented birdhouse, duly covered in camouflage canvas. He has made tents that hang from trees, pavilions for barbecues and public poetry recitals, and one for the Dutch composer Simeon ten Holt, specially designed to accommodate his concerts for four grand pianos. Whether for public or private, group or single use, the tent structure offers endless possibilities for the designer, who revels in the intersection of 'canvas architecture, design and sculpture'.

In 2001, Wapenaar developed a group of elevated tent structures and sold them to campsites in the Netherlands. But never quite satisfied with the design, or finished experimenting with the materials and possibilities, Wapenaar bought back some of his structures in 2007 and went to work on some improvements. The latest versions include a model with a 'half-height' pedestal base, powder-coated frames and cross bases that tie the separate structures together, creating enough stability so that there is no need for a concrete foundation. The designer also added some 4cm-thick oak for the decking and seating. As an intrinsic part of Wapenaar's experiments with tents is the covering material, the new tents have been covered in canvas that was specially designed and manufactured in his own studio.

These are graceful structures that fulfill the criteria for sculptural forms that Wapenaar finds essential to his work. Their bulbous shapes are like refined hot-air balloons, perching lightly on their delicate-seeming bases. But they also address another concern of his, which is to do with how people interact with each other, and the way in which tents encourage their inhabitants to communicate. 'If you set up your high-tech tent in Mongolia next to a traditional yurt, you immediately create an exchange of communication,' he observes. While at the same time, the tent, being temporary, 'is on the boundary of the private and public domain'.

The design was very much human-oriented, with the height determined by a human limit, about two metres, with an extra 60cm on top. The concept was for a family of two adults and two children to be able to sleep in one tent, and for the tents together to form a sort of 'miniature society'.

[top right] Shapes are 'boles' and 'dia-boles' with three different modules, which differ from the 2001 prototype.
[above and right] Tent interior with and without the covering.
[opposite] The new tents were erected at the Biannual in Nantes and used for overnight stays (one night at a time) and for daytime visitors.

'It is very much sculpture. It represents my ideas about how we could live with one another.'

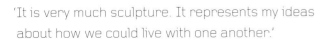

raising hopes

Bird Tower
Auburn, Alabama, USA
Rural Studio

Reuse and adaptation are in the blood of most students of the Rural Studio at Alabama's Auburn University. Launched in the early 1990s by founder architect Samuel Mockbee, Rural Studio was one of the pioneering design-build architecture programmes, and its work has inspired admiration and imitation across the globe. Their student projects are largely invested in helping the rural poor in one of the most impoverished areas of America. They challenge architecture students to design, manage and construct their own projects, often using recycled, found or very cheap materials, and to fund these projects using their own ingenuity. The Bird Tower is a recent addition to Rural Studio's projects in the Perry Lakes region, which so far have included a park pavilion, toilet facilities, a covered bridge and a baseball park.

In this area of rare hardwood forest, with a nearby hatchery helping to attract over two hundred species of birds, the construction of a tower for birdwatching was a welcome idea. But first the tower had to be taken apart and moved to its current spot. Originally constructed in the 1930s by the Civilian Conservation Corps – the domestic organization mobilized under President Franklin D. Roosevelt to help conserve the natural environment and provide jobs for thousands of unemployed men and women – the 30m-high tower was used to watch for forest fires. When the student team discovered it in 2005, the tower had been virtually abandoned by the fire service who were happy to sell it for a nominal fee of $25.00.

After being trained and certified for working at extreme heights, the students deconstructed the old tower piece by piece using only a pulley system; no cranes or other heavy machinery could be brought to the site. The pieces were then regalvanized and reassembled in their current location. New stairs were added, as was a continuous ribbon of over 152m of handrail that runs down the tower and along a 91m-long boardwalk. Both the boardwalk and the tower foundations are stabilized with a helical anchor system, which means that no poured concrete was used.

The tower now offers birdwatchers an opportunity that is unique in the continental US: being able to observe birds above the tree canopy and at levels within it from the various platforms. In an area that has been too long associated with the impoverishment of its towns instead of its rich natural beauty, the tower stands once again as a symbol of the best efforts of man to act as the custodian of his natural environment.

'The students raised money for the project by including name plaques of donors on each step and platform.'

inside outback

Permanent Camping
Mudgee, New South Wales, Australia
Casey Brown Architecture

There is something about being in a glorious landscape that inspires most people to want to make themselves even smaller so that they can be unimposing observers: rather than the fly on the wall, something like a sheep in the meadow. The aim of this compact retreat for two people is to provide a place to come and experience the wonder of the area – a sheep station on a pristine mountain in a remote area of New South Wales – that is permanent but also minimal. The latter quality has been interpreted in the true sense of the word, not as a glowing glass box with gleaming white interiors, but truly minimal in the impact on the site and intrusion on the landscape. Hence the title, 'permanent camping'.

The name could conjure images of a miner's shack or other rustic housing, and both ideas have been cleverly thought through. The structure is made permanent by secure but minimal anchorage to the ground: timber posts on steel feet bolted to concrete footings. It has also been rigorously weather-proofed with exterior flaps in corrugated copper that can be shut down when the hut isn't in use to protect it from the elements, especially seasonal bush fires. Insulation from the cold winds and searing heat is provided through multi-layered walls that are ventilated at top and bottom to allow air circulation. These are composed of timber

lining, plywood sheeting and building paper beneath the copper outer skin.

The camping idea is expressed in the very compact design which includes a sleeping loft and living area with a wood-fired stove. But here a little luxury has been tucked in, like an exquisite nut in a hard shell. The interior is lined in recycled but lovingly crafted ironbark which forms the loft and shelving and frames the internal glass doors. As the side flaps are opened up they create covered 'verandas' that expand the sheltered interior space and allow the inhabitants

to spread out a little without losing sun or rain protection. Water is collected on the roof and stored in a water tank mounted on the south elevation. A separate WC, also in copper-clad hardwood, is located a short walk to the west.

Because of the remote location and the logistical and environmental issues of transporting building materials to the site, the whole unit was prefabricated by builder Jeffrey Broadfield in Sydney, and then taken to the site for final assembly. So there is something of the sense of a temporary, moveable structure here even though it has been bolted to the ground. The materials speak not only vernacular architecture, but also the local dialect of natural colouring and weathering. Surrounded as it is by granite boulders, bush and ancient dead trees, the tower has the quality of a kids' hideout, and holds a similarly delightful promise of adventure and awe.

[opposite and right] The two-storey structure has a 3m x 3m footprint, but the sheltered area is cleverly extended when the veranda roofs are opened out.
[below] When the flaps are closed, the building is weather- and fireproof.
[bottom] The section shows the simple cubic arrangement, with the water tanks located on the building's south side.

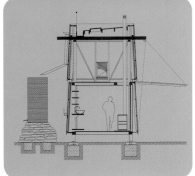

'The tower is sited at the edge of a ridge, surrounded by large granite boulders and ancient dead trees.'

alpine industry
Information Point
Mizoën, France
Hérault Arnod Architectes

Set in a steep valley of the French Alps, a protected viewing point for visitors combines the two predominant concerns of the region, according to the architects: nature and industry. Hard up against and hanging off of a stony cliff face, the Information Point recalls the trams and lifts that line many of the otherwise pristine mountainsides, while keeping an unobtrusive profile. Along a popular alpine cycling route, the Information Point offers shelter, advice and incomparable views of the Chambon dam lake. Pulling the structure up and away from the road, the architects made a virtue of the monolithic cliff face as structural support and allowed visitors to rise above the pavement level to better appreciate the surroundings.

The logic of siting the Information Point on such a narrow, elevated site posed specific challenges. The most imperative of these was that of space, so much so that even now in its finished elegance, the viewing box and stair bear some resemblance to a body pressing against the hillside to avoid cars and/or falling rock. The trunk road that skirts the project has a drop along one side of some twenty metres, and there is only a thin band of shoulder between the road and the cliff on the other side. The decision to build vertically, however, succeeds as more than just a convenient spatial solution. The neat, angular profile of rusted steel accomplishes the task of mixing the natural and the industrial. The form of a ski lift can also be discerned as the bronzed box hovers over the ascending line of the stair structure. The material contrasts in colour to the rock – though the architects say the choice of raw Cor-Ten steel was influenced by the rocks' brown colour, which itself is due to the presence of iron oxide – but melds in elemental affinity.

Below the enclosed box is a stone structure that helps support the steel construction, which is also partly embedded in the rock and strengthened on the interior with welded H-frames. It is a complement of natural and created strengths that underlies the general approach to the project, which was to somehow address a 'dichotomy' in the mountains, between 'aesthetics of integration, with the constant reference to the traditional chalet model and an aesthetic of efficiency, a necessary evil that includes cable cars, dams, hydroelectric stations, etc.'

The Information Point is functional and well-placed, and provides a convenience for tourists. Its hard form relates to that industrial necessity, but it has its own hard beauty, derived from being so well adapted to the ragged cliff face, projecting like a boulder that looks both slightly precarious and yet reassuringly immovable.

'The project seeks to create a cultural link between two
intersecting mountain worlds: nature and industry.'

[above] The glass and untreated Cor-Ten steel structure is joined to the cliff face, which rises up some 20m above the ground.
[left and opposite] From the glazed observation box, visitors have a view of the Chambon lake and valley.

rolling stock

Rolling Huts
Mazama, Washington, USA
Olson Sundberg Kundig Allen

It looks like a cross between a Modernist glass box and a 19th-century railway handcar with its crisp planes set atop chunky metal rollers, but couldn't be more at home in its wooded setting. Tom Kundig, of Olson Sundberg Kundig Allen, had already produced a robustly elegant 'cabin' for a client who wanted a shelter in the woods where he could be next to nature. The cabin, two cubed volumes of opaque and transparent planes set atop one another and offering views of wilderness on all sides, was no sprawling villa, so when the client decided he would like to share the experience with friends and relatives, he called in Kundig to create something similar in spirit on an even smaller scale.

The site was a former campground catering to recreational vehicles such as campers and trailers (RVs in American parlance), which had also been heavily grazed by horses and which the new owner intended to allow to return to its natural state. The Rolling Huts, according to the architects, 'are several steps above camping while remaining low-tech and low-impact in their design'. And they can be moved periodically to minimize long-term damage to a site. Here, 'low-tech' means suitably rustic but also highly practical. Materials include a steel-clad box on a steel-and-wood platform. The lopsided V-shaped roof is made of SIPs (pre-engineered structural insulated panels) and the glass is low E-rated. The raised platforms allow the wild meadow grass to sprout largely undisturbed, and services are located in a renovated barn structure nearby. All materials are deliberately low maintenance, inside and out.

For all their rustic charms, allusions to wagon trains and the International Style (with the architect referring to the group as a 'herd'), the huts have distinct gestures of luxury about them. The floating roofs, clerestories, sliding-glass doors and solid side (to face the rest of the 'herd'), as well as private deck and entrance are more than any humble homestead would ever offer. Each hut has more space devoted to covered decking areas (22 square metres) than to enclosed interiors (19 square metres), another aspect that in the architect's view demonstrates that 'the structures take second place to nature'.

'The huts evoke Thoreau's simple cabin in the woods; structures take second place to nature.'

[above and right] Interiors are basic, using plywood panels and cork, but have the luxury of a continuous clerestory and glazed end wall. [opposite] The exteriors, according to the architect, 'are no-maintenance materials: steel, plywood and decking'. The huts are grouped as a 'herd', though each is carefully sited towards a view of the mountains rather than its neighbour's interior.

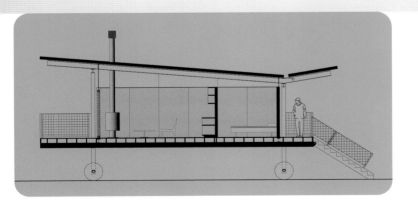

heated exchange

Floating Sauna
Hardangerfjord, Norway
Sami Rintala

Sami Rintala makes a virtue of pure forms. His Element House, set on the edge of a forest reserve near Seoul, South Korea, is an essay in elemental materials, with smaller blocks extruding from a central cube, each faced in rusted steel or wood and reaching out in some way to the natural landscape. His bridge and contemplation space in Japan also reflects an affinity for wooded sites somehow reminiscent of his native Finland.

Rintala's 2002 sauna project, carried out with students from Bergen in Norway, was closer to home and expressed a deliberate 'combining of Finnish and Norwegian culture'. The Nordic sauna may have acquired something of a clichéd typology to outsiders, like quaint gingerbread log houses, but this design shows that the beloved cleansing ritual is ripe for reinvention. The form may be a simple box, but the floating pavilion with open floor that allows for the intermittent cooling plunge in fresh (or sea) water is truly inspired. Designed to be anchored in the middle of a fjord, this little sauna craft offers privacy and freedom in almost extreme doses.

The enclosure is a simple pinewood frame with plastic sheeting for walls. Inside, an inclined bench structure provides room for the sauna-goer to sit or lie down on bare wood, while enjoying the purifying effects of heat and steam. A small stove can be splashed with water and dressed with aromatic branches while keeping the sauna appropriately hot. The translucent plastic sides offer privacy, while letting in sunlight reflected from the water. The interior can be heated to 32°C while it is a chilly -20° outside. More adventurous types can drop into the water and swim out beyond the pavilion. In warmer weather, the surrounding deck is ideal for sunbathing and as a swimming platform.

The structure was built on land on the west coast of Norway, and then floated into the fjord and anchored in place. Though the Gulf Stream keeps this part of the Norwegian waterfront ice-free for the whole year, Rintala points out that in Finland, where the sea is mostly covered in ice from December to April, the sauna should be brought ashore during winter.

'[It's about] sweat and silence, mental purification and physical maintenance.'

volcanic inspiration
Observation Deck
Pinohuacho, Chile
Rodrigo Sheward

The area of Pinohuacho in southern Chile presents a particularly heartening success story of the benefits of eco-tourism in areas of startling natural beauty and impoverished communities. After farms and villages were devastated by the eruption of Mt Villarrica in 1971, the locals were forced to rethink their approach to the land. Many native inhabitants fled to the cities, as farming – never easy in such terrain – was made impossible by the volcanic ash and lava which had rendered the soil inactive. One answer was to move cultivation further up the mountain, but as architect Rodrigo Sheward points out, 'the very action of man on that territory contributed to the devastation of what the avalanche and lava had not reached'.

What followed a few decades later has the ring of an eco-capitalist fairy-tale about it. One day the older son of a local family of woodcutters visited the metropolis of Santiago and heard of a new trend in travel called 'agriturismo'. Suddenly aware of how appealing their home would be to foreign holiday-makers, the family went to work to create an adventure camp by adding horse trails, canopy zip-wire courses, climbing and trekking trails. The extended family joined forces to make meals, work as guides and become hosts to visitors interested in exploring this remote area of the Chilean Andes.

In all, eleven families decided to invest their labour in a venture that demanded a sustainable approach to the land, but also offered the opportunity of a better standard of living. In 2006, after a year of solid work and preparation, the first paying guests arrived to enjoy the splendours of the Pinohuacho region, 12km away from the nearest village and 40km away from the nearest city, Villarrica.

While such a remote destination is heaven to the relaxed wanderer, it presents a challenge to those charged with providing the necessary shelters and equipment for their comfort, not to mention the architect of a structure sited at the highest point of elevation and 2km from a dirt track. In keeping with the commitment to the local population and the natural environment, Sheward designed an observation deck that used wood from giant fallen trees which were cut by the village woodcutter and honed by the local furniture-maker. That the design is beautiful in its simplicity seems a clichéd observation, until one appreciates the enormous blocks of wood themselves, and the vision of grandeur that rises up around it. Like the best nature huts, it pays homage to the site, while marking a small space for gazing in wonderment.

[above and below] The section and elevation show the simple geometry of the shelter. 'Steps' on the external wall provide access to the rooftop deck, while underneath visitors can shelter from rain or snow while taking in the view of the active volcano.
[right] The structure uses more than 500m of coigue pellín timber, a wood related to beech, in nearly one hundred individual pieces, some of which weighed 400kg each.

'The wood was honed on site, using a portable sawmill transported by oxen.'

off the map

Extreme climates and sites, and mobile structures

This chapter features projects that are extreme in the most popular sense, projects for which location and climate pose formidable challenges even before a brief is explored. Whether and how to attach a building to a cliff face or drop it onto a snow-covered slope are some of the questions facing these designers. Theirs is the job of not only paying homage to nature, but taking nature as a first principle before imposing a structure on a sometimes inhospitable landscape. These are places where man has dared to explore, and then return to again and again, but can never fully occupy. They include the Antarctic, where nations have claimed parcels of land for their own research purposes, but still struggle to erect shelter for long-term, year-round habitation that is still in keeping with the environmental guidelines set forth in the Madrid Protocol of 1991.

British architect Pol Taylor and his Chilean colleague Marcelo Bernal must be two of the more intrepid designers to embark on the design of shelter. Their Sala Sastruggi may resemble a basic tent structure, but it encompasses a range of materials and components that make up a highly adaptable and efficient building programme.

And they accomplish this with a minimal intrusion and residual effect on probably the least habitable landscape on Earth. Also designed for use in the Antarctic is the Polar Lab, by Richard Horden and his students from the Technical University in Munich. The group used uniform geometric volumes to create a modular unit that can be dropped in one piece by helicopter and anchored securely to ice. It is just as easy to pack up and move in case of extreme urgency.

Though they are thousands of miles from the poles, the Peak Lab and the SkiBox both exhibit the combination of daring and ingenuity that inspires good building in extreme sites. The Peak Lab, again by Richard Horden and students, is innovative both in its compact modular componentry and in its positioning, attached vertically to the side of an Alpine cliff. The SkiBox presents a much more conventional type, yet it negotiates a steep slope of the Chilean Andes with an unconventional Modernist form. Using elemental materials – local stone, glass and raw steel – the SkiBox combines elegance, nature and utility to create a shelter that would be appealing even if it were not designed to combat extreme snow, ice and wind.

Perhaps less dramatic are two projects that are sited in the branches of trees. While the local countryside is not the polar reaches or spiralling peaks, the logistics of creating a structure that relies for support on the branches or trunks of trees is a challenge of its own. For Lukasz Kos, who was inspired by the surrounding woods to create a two-storey structure that is supported by four existing trees, part of the idea was to be able to see the lake and to watch deer grazing without intruding on the scene. And for architect Andreas Wenning, the desire to build treehouses has stayed with him since childhood and through an exploration of form and materials that has resulted in a truly exceptional tree-level experiment in shelter.

From the poles to the back garden and beyond, there is no limit to where the innovative mind can take us. Gilles Ebersolt, who has explored the possibilities of inflatable structures for use on land (see XS, volume 1) and in tree canopies, has recently developed the Boomerang, which uses inflated PVC to create a shelter for use in emergencies, such as in the wake of a natural disaster, proving that extreme ideas can lead to down-to-earth solutions for basic needs.

pole position

Polar Lab
Antarctica
Richard Horden and students, TUM

Another small project with large impact from the micro-architecture students at the Technical University in Munich, headed by Richard Horden, is the Polar Lab, a temporary shelter designed specifically for use in the Antarctic. The mobile cabin provides a habitat and research station for up to three people, with storage capacity to hold supplies for three weeks without the need for additional stocks. In an area where the temperature and terrain make the transportation and assembly of materials a challenging exercise, and where workable days are very limited in number, the lightweight Polar Lab unit, like Horden's earlier Ski Haus (featured in the original volume of XS), can be deployed by helicopter or standard transportation sledges. The prefabricated station is delivered ready for use and can be quickly mounted on icy ground, using a three-point support system that takes advantage of freezing temperatures to achieve even greater stability. Once the three feet have been set into fairly shallow holes, any loose chippings will then refreeze over them, anchoring the pod securely to the floor.

The shape allows for greater volume inside, while ensuring that outside there are no flat external surfaces to collect snowfall. The angles also reduce wind resistance. Based on a regular octahedron, the module can be expanded with three additional tetrahedrons. The unit has an interior frame support of triangular beams and is fitted with eight identical carbon sandwich panels consisting of hard carbon shells on both sides filled with a 60mm layer of Prepolymere hard foam for insulation. These modular panels were expressly designed to be easily replicated in number to reduce fabrication costs. They can also be removed and added individually without destabilizing the unit.

This simple structure, say the design team, 'provides an optimal volume–surface ratio for aerodynamics, energy-efficiency, simple construction and [production] qualities'. It can be expanded to 270 per cent of its original floor area, and another 75 per cent in volume by folding down three wall panels to a horizontal position and adding further elements.

As in previous TUM projects, such as the Ski Haus, the unit sits well off the ground on its tripod support. This prevents snow from building up around entrances, and allows access to the area underneath the structure for filling tanks and other maintenance. The tripod feet can be adjusted for a slope of up to 35°. They can also be removed during delivery or 'for fast take-off in emergencies'.

'The basic idea was to design an independently functioning capsule that can be delivered in one drop.'

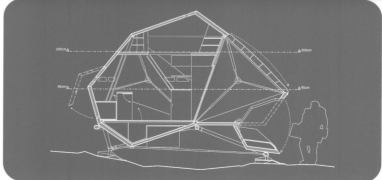

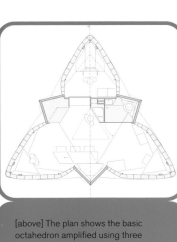

[above] The plan shows the basic octahedron amplified using three additional tetrahedron units. The units have a side length of 3m. Eight identical tetrahedron panels with a triangular inner structure are set together to build a closed capsule.

leafy perspective

4treehouse
Lake Muskoka, Ontario, Canada
Lukasz Kos

Many architects might make light of the idea of having a treehouse for their first commission. In fact, many non-architects might claim this achievement dating back some years before their professional careers. This 2003 structure, set in mature trees on the banks of Lake Muskoka in Ontario, came about not as the result of an architect's whim or childish nostalgia, but a competition. Polish-born Lukasz Kos, who studied architecture first in Manitoba, then in Krakow and Toronto, created a sophisticated, tree-hugging design that is remarkable on many fronts. Its verticality is an unexpected approach, as treehouses tend to work hard at extending floor area around trunks and branches. The idea was to go higher rather than wider, in line with the tall slender rise of the supporting poplars. The treehouse is actually a 'trees-house' that uses four standing trunks to support it.

The design itself was inspired by the 'the arrangement of trees on the site', says the architect, and it is the site that continues to dictate the experience from within it. Visitors climb a metal stair to reach the elevated shelter and enjoy views of the lake and the surrounding woodland. On land that is part of a deer reserve and includes a cottage and boathouse set within mature trees and surrounded on three sides by water, the treehouse has the genuine feel of a secluded retreat. Inside are built-in storage 'cubbies' for equipment for overnight stays, a power connection and a tap for running water. But there are no other permanent amenities, so the treehouse stays as close to an outdoor existence as possible.

As the design shows all the sympathy for the vegetation and surroundings of a dedicated native son, the structure is based on a 'traditional Muskoka balloon frame', with the vertical elements put in place first, from top to bottom and

the floors attached to the interior of the full-height structure. This method adds to the purity of the form that rises up unimpeded, showing row after row of slats across single vertical members. At night, when lit from within, it has the delicate ribbed patterning of a Chinese lantern.

It is Kos's view that by 'wrapping itself around the trees' in their existing, arbitrary location, the treehouse 'makes a formal connection with the tree growth in the forest'. The regular, rhythmic composition of slats and verticals and window openings, though very much in harmony with the forest, stands apart as an orderly arrangement of elements. But it is not an order that is too imposing or strict. The trees still sway, the wind, daylight, darkness and moonlight pass through the openings as through so many inner branches. Anyone taking shelter in its floors will certainly feel the rustle and rush of breeze. It's enough to inspire nostalgia for a child-like appreciation of things.

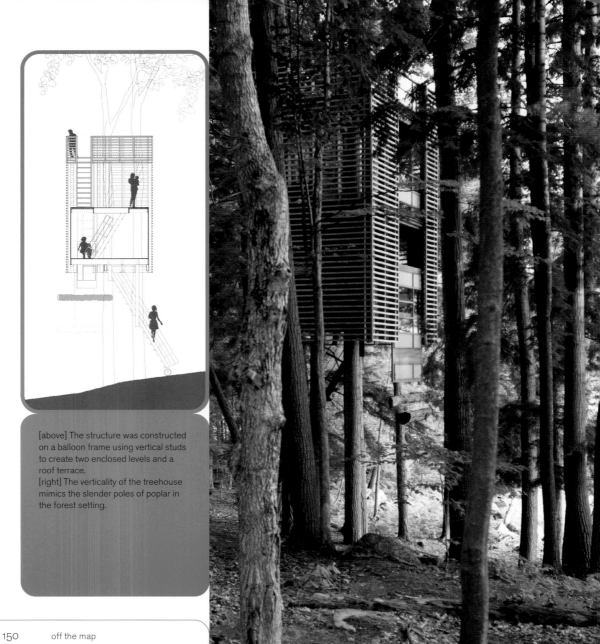

[above] The structure was constructed on a balloon frame using vertical studs to create two enclosed levels and a roof terrace.
[right] The verticality of the treehouse mimics the slender poles of poplar in the forest setting.

[left] The structural beams, joists and internal diaphragm on the first level were all made from Douglas Fir. Cedar was used for the vertical studs and clear pine for the structural diaphragm, or lattice construction.

outer spaces

Boomerang
Paris, France
Gilles Ebersolt

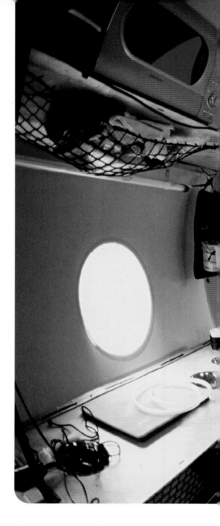

Gilles Ebersolt continues to stretch the imagination and the limits of materials by making increasingly impossible shapes with inflated PVC. Having become known for his inflatable observation rafts, as well as the Ballule (see XS, volume 1) – a transparent sphere that can be rolled down mountains while a well-insulated participant bounces along happily inside – Ebersolt is something like a birthday party balloon artist making ever more fascinating constructions out of these blow-up forms. His designs have serious applications for living, working and research, however, and, in this latest concept, for providing emergency shelter.

Never one to keep his head out of the clouds, Ebersolt looked to space travel, even to a potential human Mars landing, for ideas for a shelter that could be easily transported, quickly erected and robust in extreme weather conditions. His solution was an arrangement of inflated modules that can be adapted to all types of terrain, due to their pliable base, and anchored securely. The interior pressure is maintained by a 3,000-watt electric blower, which is used to inflate the structure, while an airlock entrance keeps the pressure stable as people come and go. The modules provide dormitory-style accommodation for up to six people, as well as a communal area for work and meals. Internal fabric hangings can be used to separate units for privacy.

All of the furnishings are lightweight and suspended from the interior walls and ceiling with high-strength cables, as are the sleeping hammocks. This keeps them secure during high winds, or even earthquakes, allowing the structure maximum movement without disruption or damage.

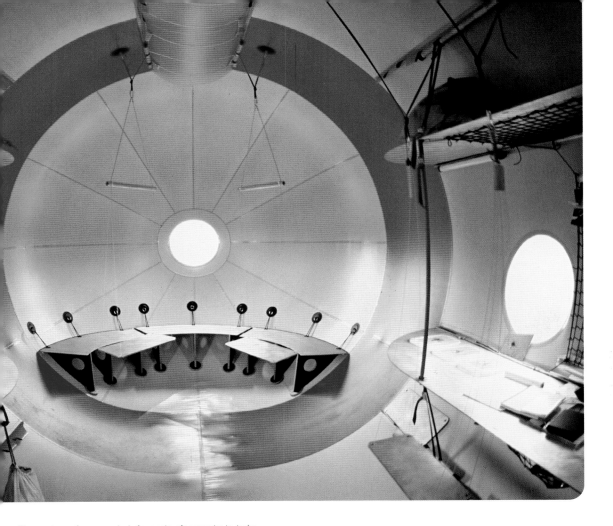

The system of suspended elements also works to help organize the interior when the Boomerang is anchored on a steep slope. Whether or not the Boomerang will go to Mars and back is still a question (up in the air?), but it may find many less lofty though more urgent uses here on Earth.

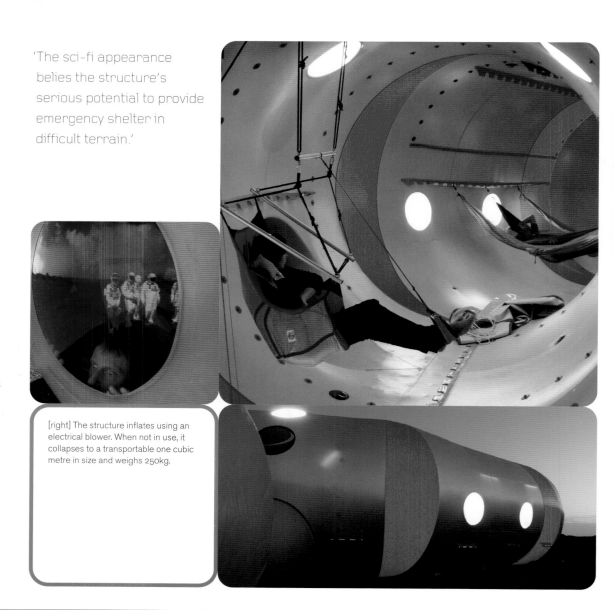

'The sci-fi appearance belies the structure's serious potential to provide emergency shelter in difficult terrain.'

[right] The structure inflates using an electrical blower. When not in use, it collapses to a transportable one cubic metre in size and weighs 250kg.

off piste

Peak Lab
Zermatt, Switzerland
Richard Horden and students

Richard Horden and his micro-architecture students at the Technical University in Munich continue to make innovative contributions to the world of lightweight, mobile and compact design. Their aims, however, are to make these structures capable of being employed in some of the world's most extreme environments. In that vein they have produced schemes for habitable stations in Alpine regions, desert plains and the Arctic; they have even worked on design prototypes that can be used in conditions of microgravity for the International Space Station.

The Peak Lab, designed in collaboration with students from both the Technical University in Munich and the Lucerne University of Applied Sciences and Art, is a building made not only for extreme weather conditions at 4,000m above sea level, but for extreme placement, hanging off a vertical cliff face. Using light construction and prefabrication methods, the designers of the Peak Lab intended to create a structure that provides areas for work and living for research or mountaineering teams. Because of its prefabricated, modular design, it will be easy to construct and demount, and should make a minimal impact on the site. Energy will be supplied by photovoltaic panels along the sunny side of the Peak Lab.

In addition to presenting a long surface to direct sunlight

for optimal solar energy gain, the vertical design has other benefits. It avoids problems of access due to build-up of snowdrifts and danger of rock falls, and has aerodynamic benefits which are crucial in such an exposed area of high winds. Using the cliff wall for support, single modules are hung, or stacked, on the frame to add levels as needed. Furnishings are integrated and also installed using this same 'hanging' system. A ladder connects the modules vertically, so the movement through them is akin to the experience of rock climbing. Small window openings on this side allow for close views of the cliff face being scaled.

As the horizontal and vertical dimensions need to be tight, the interior space needed to be optimized. This was modelled carefully on a human scale, using lengths and radii of the human body as guides, so that movement, though somewhat restricted, is accommodated in its natural parameters. Integrated furnishings are asymmetric in order to allow for areas of open movement versus seated or stationary activities. The prefabrication of the components of the Peak Lab is not only more efficient in terms of the savings in wastage and, consequently, pollution, it is necessary in such an extreme location where construction is only possible fifty days of the year.

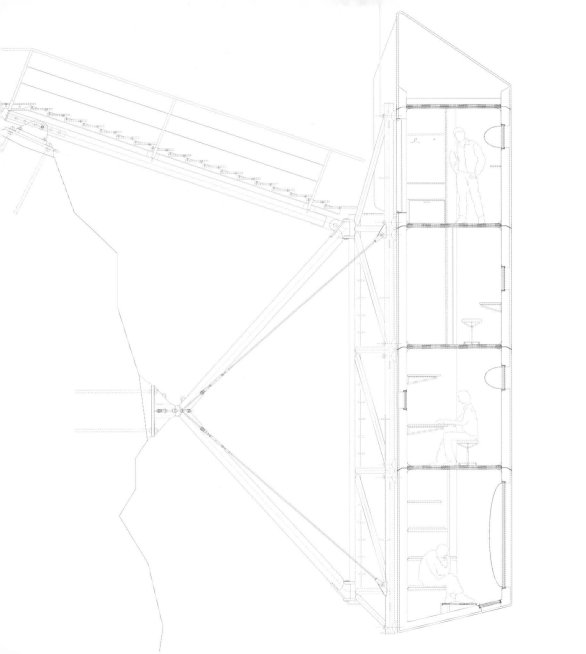

[above] Access to the Peak Lab is from a path that leads down from an observation platform on top of the mountain. The modules can be used as needed for different activities.

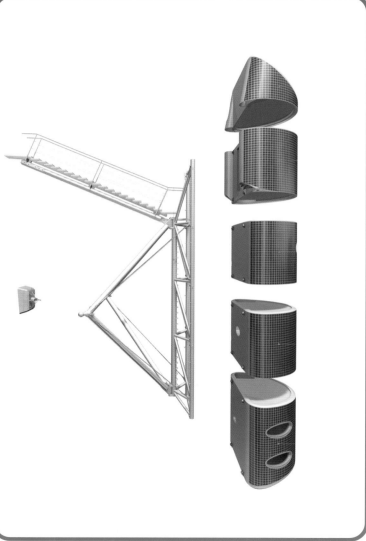

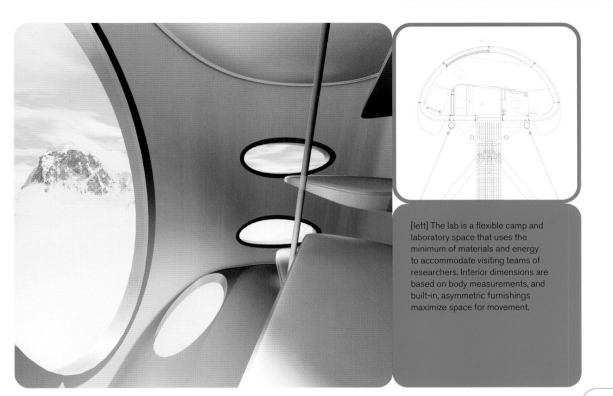

[left] The lab is a flexible camp and laboratory space that uses the minimum of materials and energy to accommodate visiting teams of researchers. Interior dimensions are based on body measurements, and built-in, asymmetric furnishings maximize space for movement.

'This high-tech, low-impact facility offers wonderful views to the Breithorn and the "copa de rolin".'

branching out

Tree House
Salzburg, Austria
Andreas Wenning (Baumraum)

To many people, architect Andreas Wenning's job must seem like a dream come true, or at least the realization of a great childhood fantasy. Wenning designs and builds treehouses – not the usual backyard variety, but thoroughly modern structures with interiors that are better designed than many a high-priced flat. His first treehouse was for himself, a work of bold geometry that resembled a wooden ark that had somehow become lodged in the tree canopy, presumably after a great flood. Since then, he has been asked to create dozens of structures, including one for a family in New York State that connects to the tree at the top of a sheer cliff face.

Despite their design niceties and interior comforts, Wenning's treehouses never lose their adventurous spirit, whether because of their height (usually between 4m and 9m off the ground) or because of their inspired configurations. Though many of his earlier structures were made of wood, this latest design is Cor-Ten steel and bears more than a passing resemblance to one of those armoured vehicles that stroll through battle scenes in the Star Wars films. This is partly due to the client's fondness for the films, but it is also to do with the architect's own design proclivities, which are readily apparent in that first tree-hung project. Here, the futuristic language is more decisive, with the solidity of the steel shell suggesting both a space ship and a submersible.

The shape has a distinctive sculptural appeal, but it also has a certain delicacy as it seems to float amidst the trees. Eight slanting stilts appear far too insubstantial to hold the cabin aloft, and contribute to the idea that this is some kind of airborne vehicle, rather than a treetop hideaway. But

appearances can be misleading, and this is a very
comfortable habitation. The interior is clean, modern and
awash in light and greenery from the many windows cut in
various angular shapes. One window at the back wraps
around the floor, affording a view of the ground below;
another has a panoramic view across the grassland to the
main house of the property. The position and angles of the
windows suit recumbent guests, who can while away the time
in a spacious 'lying area', staring up through the skylight or
into a tangle of branches for inspiration.

[above] The interior has oak boarding over rockwool insulation, and features an up-to-date lighting and stereo system. Beneath the 'lying area' and bench are drawers also made of oak. The free-standing cabin sits 4.5m above ground and is covered in Cor-Ten steel on a framework structure. The eight stilts are set on a concrete foundation.

[left] The terrace is supported by one birch and two ash trees using heavy-duty straps and steel ropes, as well as a pair of stilts. From here, the clients and their children can fish for trout on the creek below.

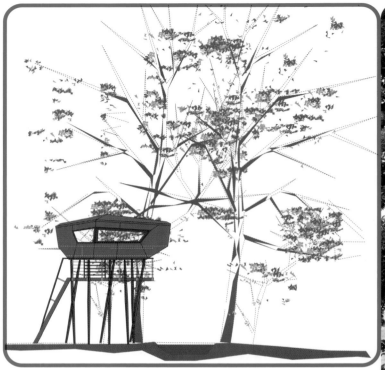

'I like the idea of being high in a tree in a small space that is rather modern.'

outer limits

Sala Sastruggi
Patriot Hills, Antarctica
ArqZe

With the exception of conditions of microgravity, the polar regions must be among the most difficult environments for an architect to address when attempting to create suitable structures for extended periods of habitation. In addition to the forces of Catabatic wind and extreme temperatures, there are strict guidelines that proscribe what is allowable in this harsh but fragile ecosystem.

Pol Taylor and Marcelo Bernal, who together form ArqZe (Architecture for Extreme Zones), have been working on solutions for EPTAP, the first permanent Blue Ice Station, which was developed in collaboration with the Chilean Air Force and deployed in 1999. The Sala Sastruggi was created as a prototype to test their Catabatic building system, which combines a lightweight tent framework with expandable modules to provide extended protective, energy-efficient space in a stable environment.

The larger Catabatic system is a flexible programme of elements designed to withstand the harsh conditions. Using a triaxial organization and double-curvature membranes, the system is highly adaptable in a place where changes in strategies and development are crucial to research and safety. As a separate but connected component to the camp, the Sala Sastruggi was built using this system to create a communal space that could be accessed from different areas of the EPTAP.

In a nice demonstration of technology transfer, the framing structure was developed from advanced yacht design. The floor membrane is highly insulated, combining laminated PVC membrane, closed-pore polyethylene and aluminium foil, and its exterior 'wings' are folded down into a trench and buried, sealing the edges and protecting them from erosion. This helps to maintain an interior temperature of around -12ºC, even when the external temperature might reach -34º. Ventilation is provided by manually controlled vents in the skylight. To further maintain a constant temperature, a rigid transparent door leads to a 'thermal exchange' chamber where incoming air is warmed before it enters the tent. Heating in the modules is achieved through electric radiant panels in each compartment, using naturally occurring energy sources whenever possible.

The Catabatic wind, which flows down some 4,000m from the polar cap to the Antarctic coast, has cleared a smooth horizontal section of blue ice that the air force use as a runway to deliver people and supplies to the area. Being aware of such power in nature in these regions will hopefully inspire more technology that is responsive to the site, deferential to ecological imperatives, and as flexible as human inhabitants are capable of being.

[below] The internal membrane is finished in a reflective surface to avoid energy losses through radiation. The Catabatic system is modular and connective. Fittings can be adapted for use on snow, gravel or rock.

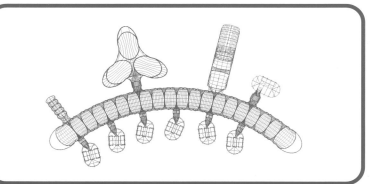

'When collapsed, the catabatic module is very compact, allowing it to be transported economically by small planes, such as Twin Otters.'

high-altitude modern

SkiBox
Portillo, Chile
dRN Arquitectos

The town of Portillo is just over 161km from Santiago and located about 2,500m high up in the Andes, and was founded around the turn of the 20th century when a railway was first pushed up over the mountains. Since the 1960s, when the Hotel Portillo was refurbished and skiing championships held in the surrounding slopes, it has become a popular holiday destination, but one that maintains a sense of fierce natural beauty. At the turn of this century, the hotel was again involved in renovation and expansion, this time with the addition of several satellite buildings that service lift stations and house facilities for ski patrols and skiers.

The young, innovative practice of Del Río Núñez were commissioned in 2006 to create one of these additions, and decided to combine an appreciation of Modernist form with features and textures of the immediate surroundings. SkiBox combines contrasting elements in a rectangular volume that in any other setting might seem like a standard Modernist box. But it is a composition of layers, like the formation of rock over millennia. And in this location against the stark landscape of snow-covered glaciers, the use of stone and glass has a direct and satisfying relation to the views of rocky peaks giving way to crystalline blue sky.

Stone and glass, together with steel, are not the obvious choice of materials for such a frozen environment, but the architects wanted to differentiate the two functions of the building through two layers of construction. The stone base anchors the building and 'unites it to the landscape', while the lighter steel-and-glass box above offers space for rest, refreshment and, of course, glorious views up the mountain. But the building is a little more complex than this.

There are layers within layers, which make clever use of natural light and work to changes in elevation. The stone at ground level is topped with a strip of clerestory windows that allows light into the basement space. Above on the next level, oxidized steel 'boards' alternate with a glass curtain wall to break up the volume and bring in light. On the south elevation, the stone 'podium' extends higher up the façade, compensating for the change in land level and creating a wrapping effect in conjunction with the steel boards opposite.

The architects say they wanted to create 'clear horizontal stratification' in keeping with the existing hotel. But the horizontality also provides a comforting vision of shelter and stability in an area dominated by such dramatic peaks and troughs. They also aimed for 'a form that had more relation with a technical container than with the romantic preconception of a mountain cottage'. While the SkiBox is certainly far from clichéd cabin typologies, it makes for a very elegant container with real local integrity.

'The inert materials – rock and steel – will age well under the extreme climatic conditions of the mountain.'

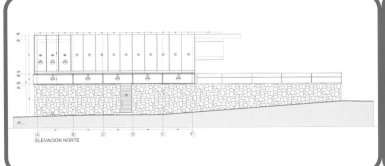

ELEVACION NORTE

[above] The stone used for the SkiBox came from the site and was worked 'without great precision'. With the oxidized steel, the stone helps the bold, Modernist volume to blend with its surroundings when the snow is melted. [left] The elevation shows the horizontal layering of stone, glass and steel above the gently rising slope.

urban
radicals

Small interventions that redefine the streetscape

The city can be a challenging place for exploring extreme building ideas. As the need to cater to growing population density comes up against conservation issues and limits of space, urban architects must constantly rethink the usual construction and design parameters if they are to improve the daily experience of the public user. Most of the projects featured here have answered this problem with mobility, while others use minimal ground space to provide shelter or services.

When UK firm Gollifer Langston began work on their Classroom of the Future, they embraced both the concepts of mobility and of minimal site demands. For these designers, the future of education is abetted by well-planned, adaptable space, so that the answer to a sudden rise in student numbers is not met by quick-fix architecture, and investment in good facilities is not wasted when buildings are vacated as the population of families with young children migrates.

Population flux and flow is also the focus of NOX-Architekten's D-Tower, but here the architects are more concerned with educating the city about the changing moods of its citizens. This is user-friendly architecture that responds, by changing colour, to the input of city-dwellers who provide information about their current mood to public computers. Looking like a cross between a sea creature and a human heart, the D-Tower takes the emotional pulse of the people of Doetinchem, and then plays it back to them in colour.

For those who want a little more anonymity, another group of Dutch designers, NIO, are attempting to create human habitation that virtually disappears from the radar. Looking like a potentially poisonous caterpillar, their Point Zero houseboat allows the inhabitant to retreat from the masses into an amorphous black hole. Danish group N55 have been working and elaborating for years on a modular habitation that would help to solve the crisis in affordable housing for the most vulnerable in society. Their Spaceframe and Floating Platform are highly efficient, easily transportable building units that can be assembled by untrained builders using a minimum of tools and requiring no poured foundations. They also work on water.

Back in the workaday context of the city, projects that aim to improve the experience of pedestrians are always welcome. In New York, GRO Architects' pedestrian route helps to mediate the disruption and discomfort of walkways near large construction sites. It may be a minimal gesture, but it speaks loudly for the walking public, drawing attention to a common hazard of the daily commute. And in Alicante, the team at Subarquitectura took the opportunity to develop a pedestrian-friendly park within an isolated traffic circle, while creating tram shelters that are small celebrations of space, light and geometry.

Space and its many possible configurations within a given volume are the preoccupations of Alex Haw, whose installation investigates the needs of the human body within the modern workplace. And space, or using less of it, is the concern of Front Architects, who have taken their cue from billboard structures to make elevated, compact living space for the single dweller in urban or remote locations. From urban to rural and back again, Gilles Ebersolt has again found building solutions using inflatable structures. His Mobile Studio is a highly flexible unit with a small, collapsible base and inflated roof structure that offers both branding opportunities and minimal space requirements. It represents a successful, if extraordinary, crossover of commercial interests and environmentally conscious design.

trailer tricks

Classroom of the Future
London, England
Gollifer Langston Architects

The UK government's building programme for schools has created a number of new and improved facilities across the country in recent years. Not all have demonstrated a good understanding of how to design a modern and inspiring space for learning. But among those making strides are the London-based firm Gollifer Langston, who have produced some of the most notable new buildings. In this, their smallest project, their focus on innovation and adaptability has resulted in something that could genuinely become a model for teaching hubs in years to come.

For teachers in the centre of London where populations are very mixed and highly mobile, the development of a classroom unit that could easily change site and function must seem like a godsend. There is, of course, precedent here. You may remember those quasi-mobile, temporary classrooms that were more like badly insulated holiday trailers and were in popular use in the 1970s. From these, Gollifer Langston seem to have taken only the mobility concept and, happily, nothing more. The design for their Classroom of the Future has all the funky, spacecraft feel of an Airstream trailer, and all the technologically advanced amenities for teaching in the 21st century.

At first glance, the interior presents a pared-down, though bold space that leaves plenty of room for specialized details. Indeed, the room is designed to accommodate recording, film and performance-based activities for a maximum capacity of fifteen students. But it also offers more than this. A continuous panel of roof lights has integrated louvres to control sunlight, either to blocking it out completely or washing the space in natural light, avoiding the atmosphere of a dark, claustrophobic enclosure. Once in place, the unit can expand from 2.5m to 4.5m wide. A ramp secures to one end, and a three-part door and panel system opens to create a porch or stage area. One of the side walls

also has an openable section that can turn the classroom into a stage or open-air pavilion.

The silver streamline capsule was, the architects say, 'fabricated using the materials and technologies of vehicles rather more than conventional building techniques'. The crossover is apparent in the choice of manufacturing firm, J.S. Fraser, a company involved in building support vehicles for Formula 1 racing. But it has more than streamlined efficiency up its sleeve. With its hydraulic ramps and legs incorporated into the chassis, the entire unit is practically self-assembled. The leg machinery, for example, raises the building off of the lorry and secures it on site. All in all, it's a building that teachers, students and planners can all be excited about.

[opposite and right] The award-winning prototype for a mobile classroom derives electricity from the host site by simply plugging into the mains power point.
[below] The chassis contains hydraulic ramps and legs for raising the unit off the transport and setting it on site.
[bottom] The section shows the unit with the ramp extended.

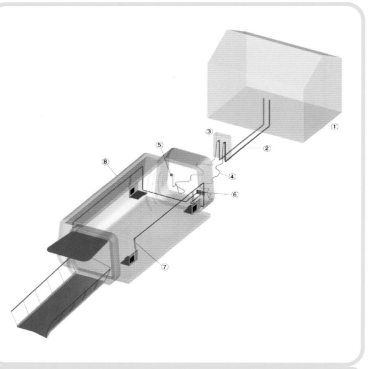

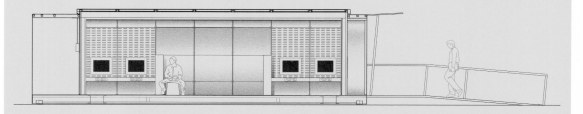

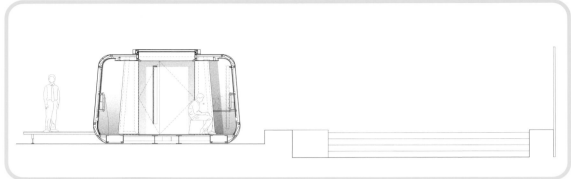

The mobile unit is expanded by opening a stage along one side, and a ramp with covered entrance access at one end. The interior includes computer stations and a large plasma screen, which can be directly linked to the computers. The open interior with curved birch-ply walls is backed by acoustic foam for sound insulation.

'The fabricator, J.S. Fraser, also builds support vehicles
for Formula 1 racing teams, including Ferrari.'

high emotion

D-Tower
Doetinchem, Netherlands
NOX-Architekten

It is architecture in three acts: a physical building, a questionnaire and a website. The public are not only asked to participate, but it is their responses to questions relating to mood and feelings that determine the appearance of the tower at any given time, on any given day. Professor Lars Spuybroek of NOX-Architekten has a wide reputation for inventing irregular organic forms and applying them to everything from public restrooms to small office spaces to major city planning proposals. Spuybroek counts the D-Tower among his 'art' works, though it is very much a building that has a roof and sides, and provides some degree of shelter.

Spuybroek also describes the project as 'a coherent hybrid of different media, where architecture is part of a larger interactive system of relationships', but it is also an extraordinary addition to the townscape. The 12m-high structure features a complex surface derived from standard and non-standard geometries, resulting in a form that recalls some sort of deep-sea bioluminescent cephalopod, with tapering limbs supporting a bulbous centre. The material is epoxy resin, shaped using a computer-generated moulding technique. Though the organic curves and glowing light resonate with nature, its surface, say the architects, 'is similar to a Gothic vault structure, where columns and surface share the same continuum'.

The process works through the responses of passers-by to a list of questions relating to 'daily emotions like hate, love, happiness and fear'. The questions were devised by Q.S. Serafijn, a Rotterdam-based artist, and the responses are graphed on the website as 'landscapes'. Those four emotions are represented by the colours green, red, blue and yellow, which are the same colours as the lights used to illuminate the tower. So observers can see from which colour is illuminated the trend of emotions in the town that day. There is also space in a capsule underneath the tower for people to place their own messages on the website 'landscape' graphs.

To make the connections run even more deeply, the D-Tower, says its designer, 'will also send prewritten love letters and flowers around from "love addresses" to "hate addresses"'. So architecture, in effect, becomes art becomes interactive community network. The number of boundaries being crossed or rubbed out with this project are like the mixed geometries of its surface. It may also function as a nice place to stand in the rain.

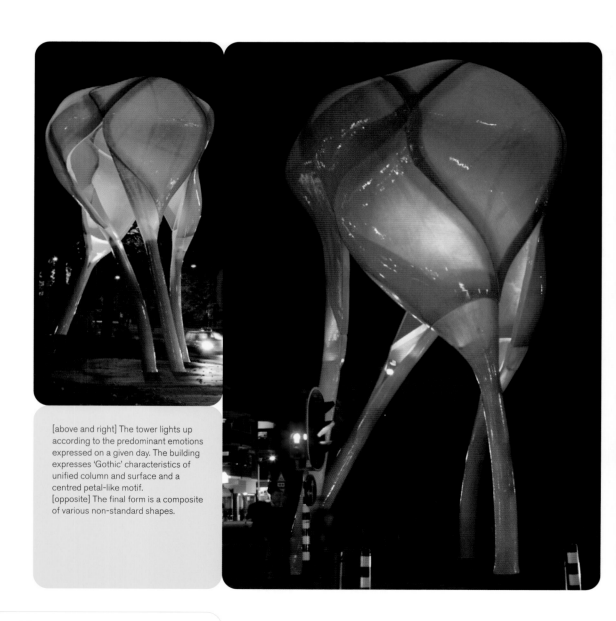

[above and right] The tower lights up according to the predominant emotions expressed on a given day. The building expresses 'Gothic' characteristics of unified column and surface and a centred petal-like motif.
[opposite] The final form is a composite of various non-standard shapes.

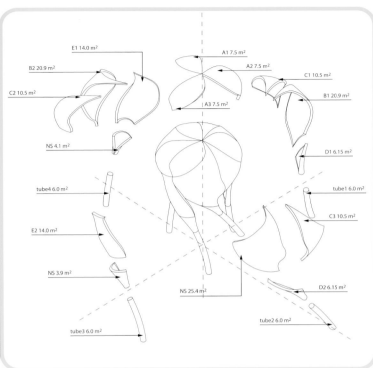

E1 14.0 m²
B2 20.9 m²
C2 10.5 m²
A1 7.5 m²
A2 7.5 m²
C1 10.5 m²
B1 20.9 m²
A3 7.5 m²
NS 4.1 m²
D1 6.15 m²
tube4 6.0 m²
tube1 6.0 m²
E2 14.0 m²
C3 10.5 m²
NS 3.9 m²
NS 25.4 m²
D2 6.15 m²
tube3 6.0 m²
tube2 6.0 m²

'Driving around in Doetinchem, one can see
which emotion is on number one that day'

blind ambition

Point Zero
Rotterdam, Netherlands
NIO Architecten

The architects describe the site for their highly unusual project as 'a seemingly impossible spot that could have come out of a book by Ballard'. Moored in the lapping serenity of the River Holendrechter, the houseboat would be placed in an idyllic scene of reeds and other small, traditionally quaint watercraft. That peaceful idyll, however, is marred by a busy motorway that crosses the river at this junction. Rather than the sound of birds, there is the roar of traffic, and darkness never covers the glare of yellow lights thrown out by oncoming vehicles. By invoking the author J.G. Ballard, the architects at NIO (Joan Almekinders, Maurice Nio and Alexander Paschaloudis) are conjuring visions of urban dystopia, but even though their houseboat design borders on some kind of organic brutalism, their aim is to mediate, not to indulge in the modern fray.

Point Zero is meant to be almost invisible, as the hypothetical mooring spot would be illegal. The name is meant to suggest both the 'blind spots', as the NIO team call them, and the gap in Dutch housing between what developers and estate agents consider saleable and more creative housing solutions, such as empty offices, disused industrial and farm buildings, caravans, and, yes, houseboats. Although Point Zero seems to be making a 'point' about housing possibilities, and about land that has been rendered unliveable by modern transportation or industry, it strives for a more formal invisibility. Its blackened exterior and amorphous shape together suggest some sort of toxic millipede, but the form is meant to be non-referential, and somewhat incomprehensible, in order to keep the structure from making any kind of statement, its designers argue.

But socio-political theories are one thing, and architecture that makes claims to solutions must deliver. In a landscape that vies between pastoral beauty and mechanical grime, the design shrinks from both, but does offer shelter, comfort, security, even luxury, inside. The necessary furnishing for the interior 'cocoon' is formed from a continuous structure that morphs from sofa to kitchen unit to second-level loft, and a polished hardwood floor covers the concrete base. The exterior may be an argument against typologies, but the shape and many dotted bubble windows create a distinctly futuristic interior. The author that comes to mind here is more the creator of The Spy Who Loved Me than of High Rise. And perhaps, even despite its deliberately low profile, Point Zero could become a highly sought-after kind of invisibility.

[above] The 15.3m x 4.0m 'cocoon' is made of sprayed polystyrene, for insulation, on a temporary inflatable mould. The outer skin is made of fibreglass, while the bubble windows are polycarbonate.

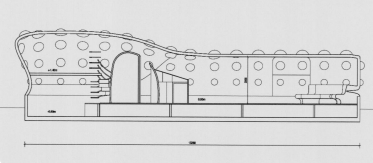

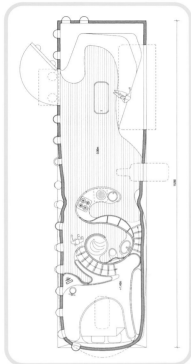

'It wants to be a "black hole", or point zero, and it tries to be invisible like a stealth [object], not only for radar but for any kind of perception.'

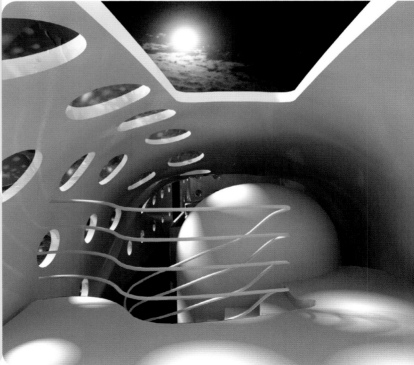

[above] The base of the houseboat is a standard concrete floating platform. The plan shows how the amorphous style carries on with the built-in furnishings and partitions scrolling through the interior.

walk this way

Best Pedestrian Route
New York, New York, USA
GRO Architects

Located in the 'extreme environment of a Manhattan construction site', Best Pedestrian Route is a play on the signs and symbols of urban construction zones, but also a very real solution to the need for protected walkways in such heavily trafficked areas of intensive building. This temporary walkway was one of three projects chosen for the 2007 RE:Construction programme, a scheme that grew out of a consortium of public and community organizations concerned with the redevelopment of Lower Manhattan. Inspired by the fact that the city was 'experiencing one of the largest public and private construction undertakings in the nation's history', the programme was set up to channel the energy of the neighbourhood's rebuilding process by 'recasting construction sites as "canvasses" for innovative public art and architecture'.

GRO Architects used the iconic orange and white colours, directional arrows and striped patterns of construction signage and route markings to create the shapes of the building elements used in their design. The stripes were cast in 3D supports with panels in dynamic, angular shapes that make an overall tilting, cantilevered structure, which protects on three sides with the top reaching upwards, making the form exciting and alleviating the usual exposed or claustrophobic effect of passing

through barriers and hoardings. This leaning form, say the architects, 'invites pedestrians to explore the instability of construction zones and the shifting boundaries between graphic symbols and the temporal dimensions of space' between building site and sidewalk.

Pedestrians can't help but notice the bold references to building work and to feel like they are part of the temporary process of construction. Instead of entirely shielding them from the building zones, it makes them participants. This notion that the structure brings a sense of community to an area in which pedestrians are often made to feel like unwanted intruders is possibly what won over the judges in the competition. If the buildings are for the people in a city, it is a good thing if the people feel included somehow in the creation of them.

The components were prefabricated off-site using CNC milling, so that the on-site assembly was accomplished in a few hours. The quick assembly is in keeping with the nature of construction barriers, but it is also part of the architects' larger drive towards the use of new technologies to enhance and move forward the relationship between designers and builders and the efficiency of construction methods. The partners who form GRO, Richard Garber and Nicole Robertson, both worked in the offices of Greg Lynn Form,

among other positions, and so their advocation of the media is not surprising. They declare their interest not only in using advanced computer technology to maximize efficiency in their own work, but to 'pressure the building industry to adopt innovative techniques that streamline and improve conventional design and construction practices while improving our built landscape'. Such large ambitions, but so far they seem to be pointed in the right direction.

'The prefabricated component parts make the assembly of this temporary structure possible in the course of several hours, not unlike the construction barriers that shift daily.'

high life

Single Hauz
Poland
Front Architects

This 2007 project is a prototype dwelling inspired by the number of people living alone in cities in the developed world, and by a desire to make urban environments more elastic in their zoning and use of space. The architects have considered the fact that, as they say, 'it seems like humankind has already discovered all the spots on the globe' – even if those spots are uninhabited, and that increasing populations naturally put pressure on housing stocks.

The young members of Front Architects, however, are convinced there is a lot of room within existing urban environments for expansion if planners and inhabitants will just consider how to live in the urban context in different ways. While historic conservation laws mean that many monolithic (and sometimes inefficient) buildings will be preserved indefinitely, and that the basic rules of planning will maintain a certain status quo, Pawel Kobrynski and his colleagues are on a mission to make planners and developers aware of the fact that cities, towns and villages are not 'lifeless creations', to be used in the same way forever.

Single Hauz takes its form from the ubiquitous commercial billboard, and creates an elevated living space for one person that requires a minimum footprint and provides a sufficient live/work/sleep area. Wiring, plumbing and water-supply systems are all housed in the structural 'leg' of the building, which is anchored in a reinforced concrete foundation. The rectangular 'house' is steel framed and covered in wood panels. The interior includes a small bathroom, living room and kitchenette, while a space between the ceiling and roof can be used for additional sleeping room for guests, a battery store, water tank, etc.

Accommodating one dweller at a time may not seem like the best way to address the need for housing large populations, but it is one way that the architects signal a rethink of housing, urban design and accepted building styles or forms. If the billboard can be reworked as housing, what other existing forms might we reconsider?

Single Hauz provides 63 cubic metres of space on two floors and is intended for use by one person. The house sits on a steel support set in a foundation of reinforced concrete. The structure is made of wood panels over steel framing with multi-layer insulated walls. Windows and doors are aluminium and high-performing glass.

'It's partly a lantern, a captain's bridge, an observation point, a secure, raised shelter.'

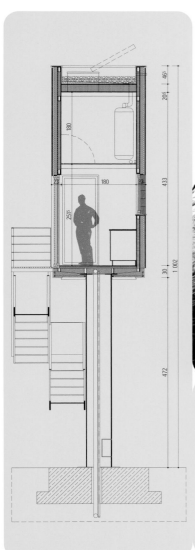

[left] The section shows the narrow arrangement of the two-level space. The Single Hauz is meant for use in a variety of settings, with all services running through the steel support.

roving reporter

Mobile Studio
Paris, France
Gilles Ebersolt

When a French television channel wanted to find a way to combine brand identity with a new broadcasting station, they turned to a designer known for making unusual structures that have been employed in some of the most out-of-the-way destinations. From the aluminium-framed ICOS that allows researchers to settle themselves and their equipment in the Amazonian tree canopy, to a raft-like apparatus that is suspended from a dirigible, also used for tropical research purposes, to the most fun you can have with a built structure going down a mountain (the Ballule, featured in the first volume of XS), the things that come out of Gilles Ebersolt's studio are nothing like the architecture of staid permanence and everything to do with inspired mobility.

With his fondness for the possibilities inherent in flexible fabrics, Ebersolt not surprisingly chose a structure that is at least partially inflatable for this project. It is a marriage of a small trailer and a highly visible, very compactable ballooning roof. But Ebersolt has controlled the form skillfully, coaxing the double-walled fabric to follow the lines of an A-frame hut. The construction of the fabric, similar in design to the Ballule, is made up of two layers of PVC sheeting held together with internal ties that are tensioned when the cavity is filled with air. The ties create a dimpled effect on the surface, but it is still, when inflated, static enough for branding effectively.

When in use, the roof is oversized to provide some side protection from wind gusts. Four translucent panels attached between the roof structure and the base give added shelter and can be lit from behind to achieve the desired effect for filming inside the tent. An additional PVC panel can be attached across the back to further enclose the space when needed. The whole apparatus folds down into its own covered trailer, which weighs less than two tons (as requested), and the roof is mechanically inflated in twenty minutes, while the entire unit is erected in under an hour. When opened, the studio offers 22 square metres of sheltered floor space for broadcasting. A sound-proofed generator maintains the interior at a constant pressure, even in the case of small leaks. For small, in-situ interviews, the mobile station provides an ideal sheltered hub of focus and quiet. But it can also be used to address a wider audience, being open like a mini-stage.

The Mobile Studio was commissioned to celebrate forty years of France's channel 3 Franche-Comté and to enable broadcasts from around the country in all weather. But given Ebersolt's penchant for going beyond the bounds of common terrestrial designs, it wouldn't be surprising to find the Mobile Study, or something deriving from it, in far more adventurous territory.

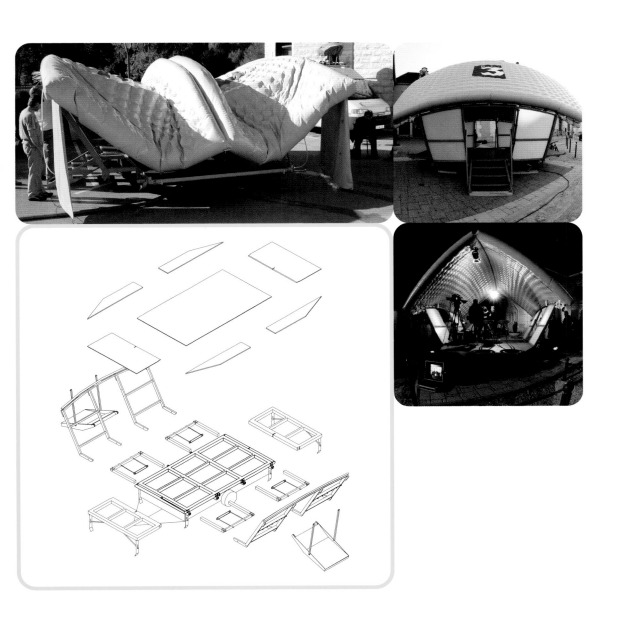

when the worker sleeps

Work/Space/Ply/Time
London, England
Alex Haw

The 2007 Urbantine Project, a competition held in London's East End, presented emerging architects with the possibility of realizing a concept as a built form, with the idea of making the process akin to product or furniture design. The brief further called on entrants to 'reflect on the changing nature of the 21st-century workplace'. Structures had to be assembled in forty-eight hours, and taken down in twenty-four. As architects of buildings of all sizes turn to the mechanical efficiency of modular components, Alex Haw seized the chance to use prefabricated parts to make spatial efficiency something of a virtue.

Haw's submission, Work/Space/Ply/Time, tries to explore all of the activities that take place in the modern workplace, including rest. To do this, he concentrated on the human scale to create a structure that maximizes the use of space, but instead of concentrating on a rectilinear volume based on the circumscribed height and reach of the average adult, it explores 'the ergonomic geometries of the human form'. A series of angular panels may not reflect the curved contours of the body exactly, but the angles have been precisely calculated not only to allow for the least amount of space necessary, but as a notional experiment to fit the maximum number of bodies into a structure at one time.

Within the overall cubic volume, ergonomic reclining or sleeping platforms are paired with integral computer workstations because, as Haw sees it, sleeping has become one of the activities that happens in busy offices like his own. Though his construction is about maximum use of redundant space, his point was to explore the 'social value of the workplace, the moments of opportunity that emerge from the relaxation it offers amongst the great mountains of focus'. Citing his own workspace as an example, he says: 'It is only efficient, or appropriate, or enjoyable, if it caters for a degree of bodily positions anywhere from vertical alertness to horizontal catatonia.' The design consists of pre-cut interlocking plywood panels that can be assembled without the use of rivets or glue – making for easy assembly and demounting, not to mention a minimum of waste.

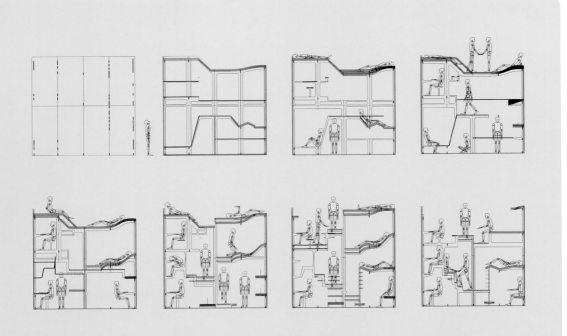

[above] Haw's design vastly overrides standard space allocations. Figuring that public desk space averages 15 square metres per desk/person, he realized that his construction (50 square metres over two levels) would only allow for about three work spaces. Instead, his 'structure sculpted by the ergonomic geometries of packed bodies' is structurally designed for 27 times that figure, or 81 bodies.

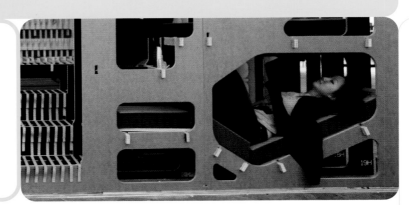

The brief was to make something that could be assembled in 48 hours and was 'roughly the size of a suburban English terraced house'. But Haw also saw an opportunity to 'ponder a future where we recognize the social value of the workspace' in an age of virtual and remote communication.
[left] A second installation of the project in Hong Kong used blackened panels and accommodated the desired quota of 81 people.

'Pavilions are always about shoving people into
a shelter of some sort of shape, but what
shape are their bodies contorted into?'

space for everyone
Spaceframe
Copenhagen, Denmark
N55

N55 is a socially conscious design collective that has spent the last decade or so challenging accepted notions of private property, living space and art. Their manifesto, expressed through both a book and 'manuals' for their designs, embraces the right of all people to basic shelter and amenities. They have explored the idea of mobile, sustainable living space in various projects, the most comprehensive being the Spaceframe, designed to accommodate three to four people. Like most N55 designs, Spaceframe is meant to be constructed by hand with a minimum of tools or other hardware, and without a cast foundation.

The components are lightweight and produced using a low degree of manufacturing. They can be easily dismounted and reassembled, so that the dwelling can be moved to a new location if needed. The basic fittings create a self-load-bearing structure using a space lattice building system, common to the make-up of crystals, also termed the 'octet truss' (patented in the 1940s by Buckminster Fuller), or 'octahedron-tetrahedron complex'. In this system, two tetrahedra and one octahedron make the basic building 'bricks' that are fitted together to make walls, foundation and roof. Apart from angled struts, there is no need for additional supports as the structure is maintained through forces of tension and compression between the elements.

Exterior material is acid-resistant stainless steel, which requires no maintenance even in wet conditions. The interior walls are covered in moisture-absorbing plaster-fibreboard plates. The floor is birch ply and the windows are polycarbonate. Space in the wall cavity can be alternately filled with insulation or left vacant to be used for storage.

The Floating Platform is built using modular construction, and allows the Spaceframe structure to be used as a floating house. Stainless-steel modules with built-in buoyancy tanks can also be assembled by hand and shaped as needed, allowing for a gradual extension of the platform area as required. Boards attached to the top of the steel truss are then topped with plates of birch ply to make the floor of the Spaceframe. The whole concept is to waste as little material, energy and space as possible, or to make maximum use of it, providing comfortable living space with a low impact in terms of both cost and environment. As proof of their belief in their designs, the members of N55 have used the Spaceframe for living and work space. But their ideas and concerns for individuals outside 'the concentrations of power' extend far beyond the complex geometries of their own forms, and the team continue to explore ways to make living space that is kinder to the environment and more equitable for society.

'There is no need for maintenance of the main construction or the outside plating. The floor and walls may need extra varnish every now and then.'

[above] The lattice structure does not depend on gravity for strength or integrity, meaning that it is suitable for use in satellites and space platforms, but the system has rarely been used for housing. The distribution of tensile forces and its ability to deform also make it safe under extreme conditions, such as earthquakes.

[left] The Spaceframe housing unit is designed to be used with the Floating Platform. Both are built using modular construction and minimal specialist tools. The Spaceframe can also be used directly on the ground without a cast foundation.

the light fantastic

Tram Stop
Alicante, Spain
Subarquitectura

As traffic circles go, this 2007 project is something of an oasis in the centre of the southeastern Mediterranean town. It is a vastly improved urban space that came about due to one of those pleasant quirks of urban planning when growth in the population and transport demands bring new life to old quarters. The commission to create a platform for a new tram stop that would link Alicante town centre with the nearby coastal towns and popular beach resorts inspired the team at Subarquitectura with the 'opportunity', they say, 'to bring back a stolen space to the city, to turn a traffic circle into a public space'. Old railway lines were being re-commissioned and a previously inaccessible island of greenery was opened to pedestrians.

The most immediate visual effect might be the Swiss-cheese styling of the perforated metal boxes used to mark the tram stop, but their relationship to the circular green space and to the nearby architecture are perhaps more relevant to the success of the scheme. The architects were also given the job of laying out the surrounding park with paths and furniture. Maintaining existing trees was a priority so the paths – designed through parametric modelling around the trees – follow a fractal pattern through to the tram shelters, providing various routes into the platforms and the pleasant sensation of a meandering park walk. The width of the paths decreases as they approach the shelter, drawing the visitor towards their destination and giving wider access at the outer edge. The size of the boxes was also a key factor in their appeal: each is the size of a tram, presenting, as it hovers over the walkway, 'an intermediate scale between the buildings and other urban elements'.

With the contextual issues so skilfully navigated, emphasis then falls on the form, a pair of rectilinear volumes that seem to float in space above the platform. The floating effect is the result of minimal supports, sited carefully at the door positions of the tram: two are slender and act in compression, two are tensed and covered in acrylic mirror to reduce their perceived mass. This apparent absence of support strengthens the visual effect of the sides, with their pattern of holes in various sizes cut into the steel exterior. Each box has the same number of holes arranged differently. Stability is achieved through the tension, increased by the number of holes, and by the cylindrical elements visible from beneath the shelter that anchor the sides together. Some of these elements are tube lighting that cast spots of illumination out to the park at night. The many perforations in the boxes also reduce wind disturbance and allow the free flow of air, especially desirable in the summer heat.

[left] The architects were asked to reconfigure the unused park contained within the traffic circle as part of the station brief. Through a fractal access system deformed in each side to avoid the existing trees, travellers can arrive from 32 different entrances

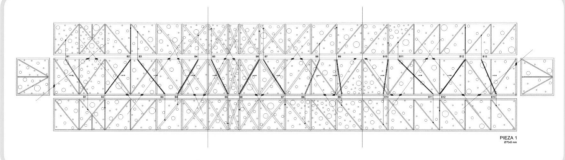

PIEZA 1
Ø70x5 mm

[following pages] The structures rely on two compressed and two stressed steel supports. Eight hundred holes in five different sizes were laser cut using CAD programming. Some holes are covered in glass, while others are left as voids. The structures are 32m long, with 22m cantilevered.

'The distribution of the holes corresponds to the normal tensions of the piece, so paradoxically, the more holes there are, the more normal tension affects the structure.'

sources

Project Credits
Architect Information
Picture Credits

project credits

Beat Wave [20]
Client: PULSE Contemporary Art Fair, Miami
Size: c. 13m x 11m x 6m (height)
Architects: J. Mayer H. Architects
Project team: Jürgen Mayer, Jonathan Busse

Bug [24]
Prototype
Size: 2.5m x 2.5m x 4.2m (height)
Architects: Najjar & Najjar Architects
Project team: Karim Najjar, Rames Najjar

Bad (Bath) [28]
Client: Akademie Schloß Solitude
Cost: c. €20,000
Size: c. 4m x 6m x 3.5m (height)
Architects: SMAQ Studio for Architecture,
Urbanism and Research
Project team: Sabine Müller, Andreas Quednau

La Estancia Chapel [32]
Client: Promotora Amates
Cost: $140,000 USD
Size: 117m²
Architects: Bunker Arquitectura
Project team: Esteban Suárez, Jorge Arteaga,
Sebastian Suárez
Collaborators: Paola Moire, Diana Arroyo, Miguel Angel
Martinez, Jimena Muhlia

Jelly Architecture [36]
Cost: $180,000 USD
Size: 10m x 3m x 5m
Architects: Gin Johannes Studio

Crisp-Packet Shelter [40]
Client: London Metropolitan University
Cost: £0
Size: 2.4m x 1.95m x 1.95m
Architect: Jack Woolley
Project team: ASD Studio 5

Glass Bubble [42]
Client: Södertorpsgårdens
Size: 120m²; 22m (length) x 10.5m (height)
x 7.5m (width)
Architects: GORA art&landscape
Project team: Monika Gora, Mårten Setterblad, Jens Linnet

Tea House [48]
Client: Museum für Angewandte Kunst
Size: 31.3m²
Architects: Kengo Kuma & Associates

Wind Shelter [50]
Client: Blackpool Borough Council
Cost: £90,000
Size: 8m (height); turntable diameter 4m
Architects: McChesney Architects
Project team: Ian McChesney with Atelier One

Density Fields [58]
Client: Materials and Applications
Sponsors: Harpo Foundation
Cost: $7,500 USD
Architects: Oyler Wu Collaborative
Project team: Dwayne Oyler, Jenny Wu, with Jian Huang,
Cory Hill, Justin Oh, Abbey Chong, students from Southern
California Institute of Architecture (SCI-Arc)

Weather Tower [62]
Client: Planungsverband Ballungsraum
Frankfurt/Rhein-Main with Stadt Offenbach
Cost: c. €100,000
Size: 13m (height)

Architects: unit-design
Project team: Bernd Hilpert, Peter Eckart (unit-design),
with Boris Banozic, Jan Schulz (bb22 Architekten)

House Dilation [66]
Client: Grizedale Arts (Adam Sutherland,
director)
Architects: Philippe Rahm Architects
Project team: Philippe Rahm, Jérôme Jacqmin, Mustapha Majid

Rolling Summer House [70]
Client: South West Forest
Cost: £12,000
Size: 3m (diameter)
Architects: Charlie Whinney Associates
Project team: Charlie Whinney with Sixixis

Tea Rooms [75]
Client: Jindong New District Constructing
Headquarters of Jinhua City
Size: 96.2m²
Architect: Liu Jiakun
Project team: Liu Jiakun, Shen Jie, Wang Wei

Reading Space [78]
Client: Jindong New District Constructing
Headquarters of Jinhua City
Size: c. 8m x 8m x 8m
Architects: Herzog & de Meuron
Project team: Jacques Herzog, Pierre de Meuron,
Ascan Mergenthaler (partners); Mark Loughnan,
Edman Choy (project architects); Wenjing Dou, Philip Fung

The Ancient Tree [82]
Client: Jindong New District Constructing
Headquarters of Jinhua City
Size: 7.4m (height); 18m (diameter)
Architects: Christ & Gantenbein Architekten
Project team: Emanuel Christ, Christoph Gantenbein,
Mona Farag (project manager), Benjamin Olschner

Bridging Tea House [86]
Client: Jindong New District Constructing
Headquarters of Jinhua City
Cost: $1,000 USD/m²

Size: built-up area 250m²
Architects: LAR Fernando Romero
Project team: Fernando Romero, Eduardo Sosa, Maria
Teresa Catrip, Carlos Bedoya, León Amezcua. Models:
Jean-Luc Fugier, Eduardo Sosa, Victor Jaime, Marcos
Betanzos, Victor Betanzos. Digital Models: Israel Alvarez,
Eduardo Sosa

M-Velope Two [90]
Prototype
Cost: $100,000 USD
Size: fully opened 4.5m (height) x 4.3m x 5.2m
Architect: Michael Jantzen

Mobile Chaplet [92]
Client: Marjorie Schlossmann
Cost: $25,000 USD
Size: 4.3m (height) x 2.4m (width) x 4.9m (depth)
Architects: Moorhead & Moorhead
Project team: Robert Moorhead, Richard Moorhead,
Granger Moorhead

Windshape [96]
Client: Savannah College of Art and Design
Size: enclosed 80m²; 8m (height)
Architects: nArchitects
Project team: Eric Bunge, Mimi Hoang, Daniela Zimmer,
Kazuya Katagiri, Takuya Shinoda, Shuji Suzumori

Aurland Lookout [104]
Client: Norwegian Highways Department
Cost: c. 17 million NKR
Size: 4m (width) x 300m (length)
Architects: Saunders & Wilhelmsen
Project team: Todd Saunders, Tommie Wilhelmsen

Boston Pendulum [110]
Client: Sustrans LTD
Cost: €92,000
Size: 9.15m (length) x 4.05m (width) x 6.25m (height)
Architects: Robbrecht & Daem Architecten
Project team: Wim Walschap (assistant), Wuyts NV (steel
construction)

Eggum Tourist Point [112]
Client: Norwegian Public Roads Administration
Size: total area, including roads and parking
spaces 5,500m²; building footprint 59m²; multi-purpose
room 20m²
Architects: Snøhetta AS
Project team: Frank Nodland, Harriet T. Rikheim,
Lars J. Nordbye, Maria Svaland

 Tent Village Revisited [116]
Client: Architect, with support from
Estuary Nantes 2007
Size: floor space 4m (diameter); tent 2.6m (height), 5m
(diameter); structures from 2m to 4m above ground
Architect: Dré Wapenaar
Project team: Technisch Bureau Cor de Heer
(structural engineer); TenCate Technical Fabrics (canvas);
Studio Dré Wapenaar (manufacturing and production)

 Bird Tower [120]
Client: Perry Lakes Board, Perry County, Alabama
Cost: c. $20,000 USD
Size: 30.5m (height)
Architects: Rural Studio, Auburn University
Project team: Natalie Butts, Paul Howard, Coley Mulcahy,
Adrienne Brady, Andrew Freer (director/professor).

 Permanent Camping [122]
Client: private
Size: 18m²
Architects: Casey Brown Architecture
Project team: Robert Brown, Hernan Alvarez

 Information Point [126]
Client: SIEPAF (Syndicat intercommunal d'études
et de programmation pour l'aménagement de la
vallée du Ferrand)
Cost: €107,200
Size: building floor area 20m²; terrace floor area 15m²
Architects: Hérault Arnod Architectes
Project team: Yves Arnod, Isabel Hérault

 Rolling Huts [130]
Size: 18.6m², plus 22.3m² deck space
Architects: Olson Sundberg Kundig Allen Architects

Project team: Tom Kundig (design principal); Jerry Garcia,
Kenny Wilson (design team); Debbie Kennedy (interior designer)

 Floating Sauna [134]
Client: Rosendal Village, Hardangerfjord
Cost: c. €1,200
Size: 9m², with floating deck 25m²
Architects: Sami Rintala with Västlands Kunstakademie
Project team: (teachers) Marco Casagrande, Sami Rintala,
Christel Sverre; (students) Kristin Lian Berg, Mona Brekke,
Simen Dyrhaug, Jenny Therese Eriksson, Mahlet Ogbé
Habte, Marja Ristiina Nickel, Ragnhild Ohma, Anne Marte
Ruud, Mona Aspen Simonsen, Thomas Aspeland Sivertsen,
Elin Solvang, Sverre Strandberg, Karolin Tampere,
Sveinung Unneland, Elisabeth Wahlström

 Observation Deck [136]
Client: European Union, Government of Chile
Cost: $1,500 CLP
Size: 25m², terrace 26m²
Architects: Rodrigo Sheward; Architecture School,
Universidad de Talca
Project team: Rodrigo Sheward, Germán Valenzuela (lead
professor); Pedro Vázquez, Carlos Vázquez, Danilo Vázquez,
Miquel Vázquez, Pablo Vázquez, Hugo Vázquez (building)

 Polar Lab [144]
Prototype
Size: 9m², expanding to 24.3m²
Architects: Richard Horden with students at the
Architecture School, Technical University, Munich
Project team: Simone Hiesinger, Michael Kehr, Wike
Schling, Sandra Spindler; (teaching team) Richard
Horden, Wieland Schmidt

 4treehouse [148]
Client: Gerald Sheff, Shanitha Kachan
Cost: $50,000 USD
Size: 38m²
Architect: Lukasz Kos

 Boomerang [152]
Prototype
Client: Bonne Pioche
Cost: €30,000

Size: when inflated 12m x 10m
Architect: Gilles Ebersolt
Project team: Denis Pegas Blanc

Peak Lab [156]
Prototype
Size: c. 2.2m (height) x 3m (width) x 1.8m (depth)
Total assemblage: 10.4m (height)
Architect: Richard Horden and students at the
Architecture School, Technical University, Munich,
and the University of Applied Sciences and Art, Lucerne
Project team: Yann Friedl, Felix Häusler, Christian Heck,
Christine Neumann, Florian Uhl, Vitus Erni, Stefan
Gassmann, Daniel Schatzmann, Christian Schmidiger, David
Schneeberger, Christoph Baumann, Iwan Plüss, Urs
Schürch; teaching team: Richard Horden, Ulrich
Pfammatter, Christian Fierz, Mathias Frey, Lydia Haack,
Walter Klasz, Armando Meletta

Tree House [160]
Client: private
Cost: c. €50,000
Size: interior 8.8m³; terrace 13.6m²; cabin
4.6m (height)
Architects: Baumraum
Project team: Andreas Wenning

Sala Sastruggi [166]
Client: Chilean Air Force, Antarctic Division
Cost: £22,000, excluding transport and installation
Size: 60m²
Architects: ArqZe Ltd
Project team: Pol Taylor, Marcelo Bernal
(engineering: ATA Ltd, Patricio Garcia)

SkiBox [170]
Client: Hotel Portillo
Size: 110m²
Architects: dRN Arquitectos
Project team: Nicolás del Río, Max Núñez

Classroom of the Future [178]
Client: London Borough of Camden
Cost: £537,000, including IT equipment
and furnishings

Size: closed 2.75m (height) x 9.4m x 2.5m; open, excluding
ramp 2.75m (height) x 9.4m x 4.1m
Architects: Gollifer Langston Architects

D-Tower [184]
Client: City of Doetinchem
Cost: €350,000
Size: 12m (height)
Architects: NOX-Architekten
Project team: Lars Spuybroek with Chris Seung-woo Yoo,
Pitupong Chaowakul, Josef Glas and Norbert Palz

Point Zero [188]
Client: Maarten Aris
Size: 15.3m x 4m
Architects: NIO Architecten
Project team: Joan Almekinders, Maurice Nio,
Alexander Paschaloudis

Best Pedestrian Route [192]
Client: Alliance for Downtown New York
Cost: $39,000 USD
Size: 12m (length) x 2.4m (width), height from 2.4m to 4.3m
Architects: GRO Architects
Project team: Richard Garber, Nicole Robertson (principals),
Patrick Candalla, Scott Corey, Philip Lee, Erin Ross

Single Hauz [194]
Client: private
Size: 14.34m², plus 14.34m² storage/convertible
space; 63.1m³
Architects: Front Architects
Project team: Pawel Kobrynski, Wojciech Krawczuk,
Marcin Sakson

Mobile Studio [198]
Client: FR Bourgogne Franche Comté
Cost: €50,000
Size: floor area, when open 22m²
Architect: Gilles Ebersolt
Project team: Gilles Ebersolt, Éric Merlo, Chrystel Courtin,
Denis Pegaz-Blanc

Work/Space/Ply/Time [200]
Client: Tent London (version 1); Hong Kong
Biennale of Urbanism and Architecture (version 2)
Cost: £13,000 ($7,000 HKD)
Size: 5m x 5m x 5m
Architect: Alex Haw
Project team: Alex Haw, Friedrich Vitzthum (project leader)
Construction team: (London 1) Ivana Bocina, Tim Culverhouse,
Rama Khalaf, Samantha Lee, Jon Lopez, Hikaru Nissanke,
Kien Pham, Emma Tubbs, Mark Rist; (London 2) Katherine
Haw, Damjan Iliev, Angeliki Koliomichu, Aram Mooradian,
Toby O'Connor, Natasha Reid; (model-making) Zamri Arif,
Charlie Blanchard, Carrie Lim, Kien Pham, Richard Prest,
Angus Lowe

Spaceframe [206]
Prototype
Cost: £15,000
Size: 8.4m (sides); area c. 40m²; 1.5m (height)
Architects: N55

Tram Stop [210]
Client: FGV (Ferrocarrils de la Generalitat
Valenciana)
Size: 36m (length) x 3m (width) x 2.5m (height)
Architects: Subarquitectura
Project team: Andres Silanes Calonge, Fernando
Valderrama Garre, Carlos Bañon Blazquez

architect information

ArqZe [166]
pol@arqze.com
marcelo.bernal@arqze.com
www.arqze.com

Atelier One [50]
9 Windmill Street, London W1T 2JF, UK
+44 20 7323 3350
mail@atelierone.com
www.atelierone.com

Boris Banozic [62]
Hohenstaufenstraße 13–25
60327 Frankfurt, Germany
+49 69 7880 7897

contact@banozic.com
www.banozic.com

Bunker Arquitectura [32]
World Trade Centre, 10th Floor
Office 19, Montecito 38
Col. Nápoles
03810 Mexico City, Mexico
esteban@bunkerarquitectura.com
www.bunkerarquitectura.com

Casey Brown Architecture [122]
63 William Street, Level 1
East Sydney 2010, Australia
+61 2 9360 7977

cb@caseybrown.com.au
www.caseybrown.com.au

Christ & Gantenbein [82]
Spitalstraße 12
4056 Basel, Switzerland
+41 61 260 9020
mail@christgantenbein.com
www.christgantenbein.com

dRN Arquitectos [170]
Isidora Goyenechea 3200
7550083 Las Condes,
Santiago, Chile
+56 2 231 4114

contacto@drn.cl
www.drn.cl

Gilles Ebersolt [152, 198]
60, rue Truffaut
75017 Paris, France
+33 1 42 29 39 74
info@gillesebersolt.com
www.gillesebersolt.com

Front Architects [194]
ul. Lechicka 59
61-695 Poznan, Poland
+48 618 226 781
biuro@frontarchitects.pl
www.frontarchitects.pl

Gollifer Langston Architects [178]
48 Poland Street
London W1F 7ND, UK
+44 20 7734 2134
info@gollifer.co.uk
www.gollifer.co.uk

Monika Gora [42]
Vilebovägen 4a
21763 Malmö, Sweden
+46 40 911 913
info@gora.se
www.gora.se

GRO Architects [192]
7 Dey Street, Suite 1102
New York, New York 10007, USA
+1 212 346 0705
richard@groarc.com
nicole@groarc.com
www.groarc.com

Alex Haw [200]
14 Bacon Street
London E1 6LF, UK
+44 7815 040 619
atmos.studio@gmail.com
www.atmosstudio.com

Hérault Arnod Architectes [126]
16, rue Thiers
38000 Grenoble, France
+33 4 76 12 94 94
zzz@herault-arnod.fr
www.herault-arnod.fr

Herzog & de Meuron [78]
Rheinschanze 6
Basel, Switzerland
+41 61 385 5757
info@herzogdemeuron.ch

Richard Horden [144, 156]
Technical University, Munich
Arcisstraße 21
80333 Munich, Germany
+49 89 289 01
http://portal.mytum.de

J. Mayer H. [20]
Bleibtreustraße 54
10623 Berlin, Germany
+49 30 3150 6117
contact@jmayerh.de
www.jmayerh.de

Michael Jantzen [90]
+1 310 989 1897
info@michaeljantzen.com
www.michaeljantzen.com

Gin Johannes [36]
571-9 Mamiya Kannami
Tagata, Shizuoka 419-0123, Japan
+81 50 1238 9050
ginjohannes@ybb.ne.jp
www.geocities.jp/ginjohannes

Lukasz Kos [148]
917 Lincoln Boulevard, Unit B
Santa Monica, California 90403, USA
+1 310 230 5007
office@studiolukaszkos.com
www.studiolukaszkos.com

Kengo Kuma [48]
2-24-8 BY-CUBE 2F Minami-Aoyama
Minato-ku, Tokyo 107-0062, Japan
+81 3 3401 7721
kuma@ba2.so-net.ne.jp
www.kkaa.co.jp

Liu Jiakun [75]
2-7F, Block 11, 3 Yulin Nanlu
Chengdu, Sichuan
610041 China
+86 28 8558 9491
jkads@263.net
www.jiakun.com

Ian McChesney [50]
1A Iliffe Street
London SE17 3LJ, UK
+44 20 7703 1133
design@mcchesney.co.uk
www.mcchesney.co.uk

Moorhead & Moorhead [92]
83 Canal Street, #309
New York, New York 10002, USA
+1 212 219 8489
info@moorheadandmoorhead.com
www.moorheadandmoorhead.com

N55 [206]
n55@n55.dk
www.n55.dk

Najjar & Najjar [24]
Seidlgasse 41/5a
1030 Vienna, Austria
+43 1 595 3408
office@najjar-najjar.com
www.najjar-najjar.com

nArchitects [96]
68 Jay Street, #317
Brooklyn, New York 11201, USA
+1 718 260 0845

n@narchitects.com
www.narchitects.com

NIO Architecten [188]
Schiedamse Vest 95a
3012 BG Rotterdam, Netherlands
+31 10 412 2318
nio@nio.nl
www.nio.nl

NOX-Architekten [184]
Postbus 620
3000 AP Rotterdam, Netherlands
+31 10 477 2853
info@noxarch.com
www.noxarch.com

Olson Sundberg Kundig Allen [130]
159 South Jackson Street, Suite 600
Seattle, Washington 98104, USA
+1 206 624 5670
newinquiry@oskaarchitects.com
www.oskaarchitects.com

Oyler Wu Collaborative [58]
2404 Wilshire Boulevard, 9D
Los Angeles, California 90057, USA
+1 213 736 1277
info@oylerwu.com
http://oylerwu.com

Philippe Rahm [66]
12, rue Chabanais
75002 Paris, France
+33 1 49 26 91 55
info@philipperahm.com
www.philipperahm.com

Sami Rintala [134]
www.samirintala.com

Robbrecht & Daem [110]
Lieremanstraat 64
9000 Ghent, Belgium
+32 9 216 2630
www.robbrechtendaem.com

Fernando Romero [86]
General Francisco Ramírez 5B
Col. Ampliación Daniel Garza
11840 Mexico City, Mexico
+52 55 2614 1060
lar@laboratoryofarchtecture.com
www.lar-fernandoromero.com

Rural Studio [120]
College of Architecture,
Design & Construction
School of Architecture,
104 Dudley Hall, Auburn University
Alabama 36849, USA
+1 334 624 4483
rstudio@auburn.edu
www.cadc.auburn.edu/soa/rural-studio

Todd Saunders [104]
Vestre torggate 22
5015 Bergen, Norway
+47 55 36 85 06
post@saunders.no
www.saunders.no

Rodrigo Sheward [136]
rodrigosheward@gmail.com
http://pinohuacho.blogspot.com

SMAQ [28]
C. Beersmansstraße 5D
3025 EA Rotterdam, Netherlands
+31 10 452 0032
mail@smaq.net
www.smaq.net

Snøhetta Architects [112]
Skur 39, Vippetangen
0150 Oslo, Norway
+47 24 15 60 60
contact@snoarc.no
www.snoarc.no

Subarquitectura [210]
Av. de la Estacion 8. 7A

03005 Alicante, Spain
+34 965 135 914
www.subarquitectura.com
www.subarquitectura.com

unit-design [62]
Holbeinstraße 25
60596 Frankfurt, Germany
+49 69 6605 7880
info@unit-design.de
www.unit-design.de

Dré Wapenaar [116]
Vaandrigstraat 10
3034 PX Rotterdam, Netherlands
info@drewapenaar.com
www.drewapenaar.com

Andreas Wenning [160]
Roonstraße 49
28203 Bremen, Germany
+49 4 2170 5122
a.wenning@baumraum.de
www.baumraum.de

Charlie Whinney [70]
+44 7785 317 014
info@charliewhinney.com
www.charliewhinney.com

Tommie Wilhelmsen [104]
Grannestunet 12
4052 Røyneberg, Norway
+47 917 444 76
tommie@online.no
www.tommie-wilhelmsen.no

Jack Woolley [40]
38 Thornhill Square
London N1 1BE, UK
+44 7773 325 688
jack@woolley.org.uk

picture credits